SECRETS OF LIVING

Eternal Fountain of Inspiration in Bhagavad Gita

Goddess Saraswati blesses the right education in all of us.

SECRETS OF LIVING

Eternal Fountain of Inspiration In Bhagavad Gita

Rajiv Sachdev
Neeraj Gupta

Foreword by

Dr. Karan Singh
Mary Pat Fisher

Sterling Paperbacks

STERLING PAPERBACKS
An imprint of
Sterling Publishers (P) Ltd.
A-59, Okhla Industrial Area, Phase-II, New Delhi-110020.
Tel: 26387070, 26386209; Fax: 91-11-26383788
E-mail: mail@sterlingpublishers.com
www.sterlingpublishers.com

Secrets of Living
Eternal Fountain of Inspiration in Bhagavad Gita
© 2011, Rajiv Sachdev and Neeraj Gupta
ISBN 978 81 207 6658 7

All rights are reserved.
No part of this publication may be reproduced, stored in a retrieval system or transmitted, in any form or by any means, mechanical, photocopying, recording or otherwise, without prior written permission of the author.

Printed in India
Printed and Published by Sterling Publishers Pvt. Ltd., New Delhi-110 020.

Dedicated in the loving memory of my parents

Foreword

The Bhagavad Gita, along with the Bible and the Quran, is one of the three most widely circulated spiritual texts in the world. Although the supreme shastras of Hinduism are the *Upanishads*, over the centuries the Gita has become the most popular Hindu text as also a widely read book for all those interested in spiritualism, religion and the interfaith movement. Along with the Upanishads and the Brahmasutras, the Bhagavad Gita is one of the three foundations of the Vedanta, and all great philosophers and thinkers from Adi Shankaracharya down to Sri Aurobindo, have written commentaries on these three texts to substantiate their particular point of view. It is for that reason that we have a large number of commentaries on Gita written from different philosophical viewpoints.

Adi Shankaracharya in one of his *stotras* says that even a little knowledge of the Gita can free us from the fear of death, and the Gita itself says – *swalpmapyasya dharmasya trayate mahato bhayat*-- Even a little of this dharma saves from a great fear. Fearlessness, therefore, seems to be a keynote of the Gita and in fact, the last words of Sri Krishna are –*ma shuchah*– fear not.

The popularity of the Gita can be traced to four unique factors. The first is that the Gita is a scripture of conflict. Unlike the Upanishads, which are spoken in a very calm and serene atmosphere with the *Guru* seated and one or more disciples seated around him on the banks of a river or on a mountain-side, the Gita setting is in the midst of a fratricidal war between two branches of the Kuru clan. Both the armies are arrayed, conches have sounded and the battle is just about to begin when the Gita is revealed. Today we find ourselves in a conflictual situation. Despite great progress, humanity is still in the throes of multiple battles, and therefore Krishna's exhortation to *Arjuna* to arise and fight resonates within all of us. However, we must remember that the fight is not simply for Arjuna's ego, or even for the victory of the *Pandavas*. The challenge is to become a warrior for the divine cause, a fighter for the divine destiny. This call to arms is therefore something which appeals to all of us.

The second unique feature of the Gita is the extraordinary personality of Sri Krishna. The Upanishads contain many great gurus and disciples, but in the Gita it is Lord Krishna himself who is speaking and hence his words have a special authority. In the course of the Gita, Sri Krishna makes it clear that it is not simply as an individual that he is speaking but as representative of the divine power itself, hence the teachings of the Gita make a special impact on our minds.

The third reason for the Gita's popularity revolves around the extremely close and holistic relationship between Krishna and Arjuna. In a beautiful verse after Arjuna gets the *vishwaroop darshan*, the all embracing vision of the Divine, Arjuna says "I prostrate before you and demand grace from you, as a father to a son, and as a friend to a dear comrade and as a lover to the beloved." Although the Guru-Shishya relationship is central to the entire Hindu teaching, no where it is more integral than between Krishna and Arjuna. Krishna's voice is not simply emanating from a seventh heaven to a trembling disciple below, but rather a dialogue suffused with love, compassion and understanding. This factor makes a special impact upon us today, besieged as we are by inner and outer conflicts and tension.

Fourthly, the reason for the Gita's extraordinary popularity is that its teaching are directed not towards any particular caste, or creed or race or nation. They are in fact addressed to the entire humanity, and Krishna explicitly says that in whatever way people worship him, he will make that faith strong. This echoes the ancient Rig Vedic concept of – *ekam sad viprah bahudha vadanti* – the truth is one the wise call it by many names.

As I have said, there have been numerous commentaries and interpretations of the Gita. The present effort is by two young IT professionals – Rajiv Sachdev and Neeraj Gupta. They have interpreted the Gita by presenting it in five sections for which they have chosen verses from the entire text. The book also contains some attractive pictures and diagrams, which will make it popular, particularly among young professionals. I commend them for the devotion with which they have produced this book, and wish them well in the future.

9 June 2011 **Karan Singh**

President, Indian Council for Cultural Relations (ICCR)
and Member of Parliament

Foreword

It is a very promising sign of our times that two executives from IT have dedicated themselves to creating a new commentary on the sublime Bhagavad Gita. As people trained in logical thinking, they have approached the Science of the *Soul* very systematically and rationally, and have set forth its eternal teachings as having irresistible logic.

At the same time, their love for God shines throughout their commentary and draws forth desire for God realisation in the reader.

Rather than following the traditional sequence of the verses, the authors have attempted to draw out the basic themes. Thus in one section they first quote and explain a verse from Chapter 2 which describes the process by which anger leads to delusion, which leads to bewilderment of memory, leads to loss of intelligence, which can make one sink again into the pool of materialism.

Then as a corollary, they explore a verse from Chapter 16 which speaks of lust, anger, and greed as the gates to hell.

Moving here and there throughout the classic text, they gradually paint a complete picture of the journey of the soul through many births and present compelling arguments for overcoming negative tendencies and devoting oneself wholeheartedly to God.

This book intentionally speaks to ordinary people trying to survive in the modern world. Again and again, they emphasise the central teaching of the Bhagavad Gita, which is to perform one's proper duties without any attachment to the fruits of one's actions and with understanding that God's system is at work in everything.

The authors speak directly to professional people like themselves when they write:

> "Your work should be pure, your actions should help people, you should be humble, you should be approachable, and you should be devoting your duty to make His world more beautiful, truthful and trustworthy.
>
> People working with you should love you from the heart, should respect you from the heart. Your money spending decisions should be good for the people working for you and for the society."

They also quote various passages in which Lord Krishna promises that those who do their duties without attachment and also meditate on God will quickly rise towards God's home. To wealthy people, they make this valuable suggestion: "You do not need to leave your home and live in a smaller home or a forest but you need to change the environment of your home so that God is ready to come to your home."

As they further explain through passages from the Gita, "Love is remembering Him all the time, and when that stage is reached, you will feel the lightness and you will understand what pleasure actually means and how different is it from this material world."

This volume speaks to all who have taken human birth, with their varying *karmas*, their varying tendencies towards

Sattvika, Rajasika, or *Tamasika* ways, and shows all how to move from where they are now towards the ultimate goal of life, as defined by the Bhagavad Gita: liberation from all lower transient realms, leading to eternal life of the soul in God's home.

10 May, 2011 **Mary Pat Fisher**
Director
Gobind Sadan Institute for
Advanced Studies in Comparative Religion
New Delhi

A special message

I met Rajiv Sachdev and Neeraj Gupta first time in New Delhi. They showed me the book they had written on Bhagavad Gita.

I have seen this book and found extremely useful for any one who is interested in Lord Krishna's messages and spiritual journey. I am very happy to see these messages of Bhagavad Gita going out to all the readers around the world where a deserving person can come close to Krishna, which is what the final destination of human life is, i.e. "Going back home".

I wish them all the best in spreading Krishna's message around the globe.

Vinod Agarwal
Krishna Bhajan Singer
Mumbai

Acknowledgements

My father left his human body in 2001 and my mother in 2006. I dedicate this book to their remembrance. My parents were devotee of Lord Radha – Krishna, Maa Durga and Bhagavad Gita. My parents installed many idols at Maa Adhya Shakti Dham, Sector 16, Rohini, New Delhi. The pictures of those idols have been given in this book.

I am thankful to my family – Anu (Wife), Vanshika (Daughter), Ramit (Son), and my brother Rajesh for their support in making me fulfill this wonderful dream of mine.

Neeraj and I would like to thank Dr. Karan Singh and Mary Pat Fisher for reviewing and writing foreword for our book. We would also like to thank Shri Vinod Agarwal for his guidance and encouragement towards writing this book.

Preface

I read complete Srimad Bhagavad Gita first time in 1981 when I was in the fourth year of Engineering at *Kurukshetra*. Since then I have gone over the Holy Scripture possibly a few hundred times. Over the years, I started realising the deep messages hidden in the words and verses of this Holy Scripture.

After a beautiful dream of Lord Radha-Krishna and Maa Durga, we got an encouragement that Lord Krishna's messages should be shared with more and more people. I shared my thoughts and some of the compilations with Neeraj. Together we decided to compile all the work and understanding into a book. Neeraj and I strongly believe that inspiration to understand, write and compile all this work has happened only with the blessings of Lord Radha-Krishna and Maa Durga.

Life is short, before one understands the rules of the life, the whistle is blown and one is called back by God. Material game is over and we enter into God's world (the spiritual world). We feel no one taught us the rules of the Game, may be we missed reading out those rules or understanding from one who wanted to teach us – Our Parents , Our Guru , Our elders and our holy scriptures.

We defined our own rules for the life game and we declared ourselves as the winner only to find the truth at the time of death that the rules were different. Time will make us history.

We have seen many loved ones departing in our presence, yet their death failed to engrave the message of death that we will also be no more one day. It is difficult to convince a person that he or she will die one day.

Time plays a major role in our life and brings us closer to death every moment yet we never understand, appreciate and feel the presence of Time. If one knows that he will die and it does not bring any change in him, then he has a hard task ahead. It means the message of death just goes to intelligence but fails to bring in any change in his lifestyle. For a God realised soul, message of death is a new message every day which governs him on what to do and what not to do. It reminds him on the right rules of the journey as prescribed in scriptures.

This book is based on teachings from Bhagavad Gita which teaches us "How to live and How to Die". It tells us about the Life after Death. It teaches us about the Life before we were born which brought us to our current family and environment.

This book is about the karmas (actions in life) and how do they change our life now and also after death.

Message of Bhagavad Gita was given by Lord Krishna in the battlefield of Kurukshetra around 5000 years back. Krishna taught Bhagavad Gita to Arjun on the first day of the battle in the battlefield when Arjun decided not to engage in righteous war. Krishna guided him on his duty and importance of karmas and he decided to engage in the righteous war for the welfare of the human race.

Bhagavad Gita has been narrated by Lord Krishna and that makes the whole difference. This is one of the rare books that had been narrated by God, so the book itself is God as well as Guru. Messages in Bhagavad Gita may seem simple if read with intelligence. But if the intelligence communicates the messages to Mind, then the messages are very deep and can bring in desired changes in any individual.

One's birth in a particular family, status of the family, environment around the family, country of birth is not incidental. It is the result of cumulative karmas of the individual over last many births. Anger, Ego, Desire – these three feelings in an individual are not incidental, these have been brought forward from previous births and will be carried forward to one's next birth with whatever change one brings in them during this lifetime. Our karma only will decide our destination after death. Our previous karmas only decided our current birth and the environment.

One may have a lot of planning in life. What is going to override our planning is God's planning. His planning is no different than what we earned based on our karmas of last few births, so basically it is our own planning and achievements. What will work best for any individual in any environment is to take shelter under Him (The Lord) and work under the guidance of the Almighty (Follow his teachings mentioned in the scriptures).

We write our own destiny, not God. It is a just, fair and well-defined system of God that guides us to the way to our next birth. It may not be easy to get this human birth again. It may look obvious but it is not.

One should not lose hard earned breaths of this life in worldly enjoyments that will die one day and we will also not be able to enjoy these material pleasures beyond a day because our body will not support us for these worldly enjoyments. One needs to think about the life after death during his present life and hence focus on the right karmas.

After death, some may merge in the Almighty which is all peace, some may return as human beings on this earth and some may go to the lower worlds of animals, insects and birds.

This book has some of the selected verses (*shlokas*) from Bhagavad Gita and their messages have been interpreted in today's context in simple and easy language. We all influence lot of lives in our family, society, place of work and friends. We can do this in different ways and that is what makes the difference between a material sensitive person and God realised soul.

The teachings do not differ from religion to religion. Many *avatars* descend from the same Almighty and go back.

We worked together for many months to give a shape to this book which is basically a collection of the messages of Lord Krishna in Bhagavad Gita. We have a dream that this work of Lord Krishna's messages will bring a change in many lives, as more and more people focus on the righteous karmas.

Rajiv Sachdev

Neeraj Gupta

Contents

Foreword by *Dr. Karan Singh*	7
Foreword by *Mary Pat Fisher*	10
A special message from *Vinod Agarwal*	13
Acknowledgements	14
Preface	15

Section 1 – God decides whom to meet

• Scriptures should be followed instead of defining our own rules	25
• God decides whom to meet	27
• A deserving person will listen about soul and God (Oversoul)	31
• Lord says – I am spiritual science of the self (Soul)	33
• God lives above Time	34
• Soul that keeps us alive belongs to God (Oversoul)	38
• Your true identity is your soul and soul never dies	40
• Soul remains pure even if karmas are not pure	43
• Soul inside us is always connected to God	44
• God is creator of love and He loves you more than you do	46
• Connect intelligence and mind (through meditation) to reach the soul	49

- Intelligence and meditation help control the wandering mind 54
- Anger – Ego – Desire are three gates to hell 58

Section 2 – Heaven is not on the way to God's home

- The consciousness of a God realised soul is different than a materially engrossed person 63
- Heaven is not on way to God's Home 64
- God does not decide your actions, nature influences actions 69
- As you sow, so shall you reap 73
- Even intelligent men have little or no control on their nature 75
- God takes birth from time to time with a purpose 77
- Overall environment deteriorates from satyug to kaliyug 79

Section 3 – Death migration process

- Soul carries intellect, mind, senses to the new body after death 83
- Three destinations after death – higher worlds, human birth or lower worlds 86
- Devoted soul that fails to reach God in current life gets more promising environment in next life for liberation 90
- If you die as an angry person, you will be born as an angry person 95
- Anger – Ego – Desire promote each other but the determined soul (one in thousand) can overcome his anger 97
- A learned soul sees God in everyone 100

Section 4 – God's planning will overrule your planning

- God realised soul gets knowledge from within 105
- Self Evaluation – Where one is heading after death 107
- Domination of modes at the time of death decides the next birth 117
- Surrender to God for renunciation 121
- Embrace your current environment whole heartedly 124
- You can reach God within this life 125
- God is always working 126
- God's planning will overrule your planning 129
- Internal purification is must to start the journey towards God 134
- The power of internal purity 139
- To reach God one should meditate while performing all his duties 141
- Karmayoga and renunciation will take you to God's home 145
- Perform all actions keeping maintenance of the world order in mind 147
- Worship of Lord Krishna is a complete worship 148
- Worshipping decides different destinations 151
- Krishna showed Vishnu form to Arjun 152

Section 5 – Failure is also success on His path

- Failure is also success on His path 155
- It is easier for a committed Karmayogi to reach God 160
- Destiny (Latencies of past actions) – an important compelling influencer in your life 162

- Actions driven by ego should not be confused as destiny — 165
- Maya is always pulling towards material world, only God's blessings will help — 166
- Sattvika and renunciation together help in liberation — 168
- General qualities of a devotee entitled to merge with God — 169
- God loves one who neither hurts nor gets hurt — 172
- Jaap yagya is supreme yagya for liberation — 173
- All sacrifices take you closer to God — 176
- All actions except sacrifice bind you…..also follow give back — 178
- Samatava Yoga – evenness of mind in success and failure–way to God — 180
- One's biggest enemy and one's best friend is one himself — 181
- God will step in to help you if you fail to invoke the inner self — 182
- True knowledge is seeing Him in everything — 184
- Gayatri Mantra — 185
- Hare Krishna Mahamantra — 187
- *Ekadshi Fast* – Fast for Krishna — 188
- Gokul - 84 *khamba* and cows of Nand Baba — 190
- Goddess Durga and Goddesss Mahalaxmi is creation of all Gods and worlds — 191
- Radha is consort of Lord Krishna — 193
- *Tulsi* is worshipped in every hindu family — 194
- *Glossary* — 195

Section -1

God decides whom to meet

Sri Radha – Krishna

Scriptures should be followed instead of defining our own rules

> Discarding the injunctions of the scripture, he who acts in an arbitrary way according to his own sweet will, such a person neither attains occult powers, nor the supreme goal nor even happiness.
>
> जो पुरुष शास्त्रविधिको त्यागकर अपनी इच्छासे मनमाना आचरण करता है, वह न सिद्धिको प्राप्त होता है, न परमगतिको और न सुखको ही ॥
>
> Chapter 16 – verse 23

Bhagavad Gita was taught by Lord Krishna to Arjun in the middle of the battlefield when the two forces were standing face to face waiting for the signal to start the war. 5000 years back Battle of Mahabharata was fought in the fields of Kurukshetra. Rules for the war were well defined like starting the war with a signal and ending the war with sunset. Arjun was the key warrior of Pandavas and Lord Krishna was driving his chariot. The battle was fought on horses.

Arjuna saw his cousins, well wishers, grandfathers, fathers-in-law, Guru and many respected relations on the opposite side. He became very emotional and decided not to engage in the fight for the kingdom and preferred to live the life as a beggar. That is the time when Lord Krishna revealed Bhagavad Gita to Arjun right in the middle of the battlefield.

Arjuna was not able to decide what was the right thing to do. Lord Krishna told him, "In this time of deciding what is right and what is not, I will explain to you what the scriptures say. Do not decide on your own what is right and what is not."

That is one of the reasons that Bhagavad Gita is the most read scripture in the world even today as it teaches you what is the right thing to do – how to live and how to die. Normally we decide with our intelligence on what is right and that is where normally we go wrong. We must follow the scriptures and that is in short we have tried to cover in this book.

> Therefore, the scripture alone is your guide in determining what should be done and what should not be done. Knowing this, you ought to perform only such action as is ordained by the scriptures.
>
> इससे तेरे लिये इस कर्तव्य और अकर्तव्यकी व्यवस्थामें शास्त्र ही प्रमाण है। ऐसा जानकर तू शास्त्रविधिसे नियत कर्म ही करनेयोग्य है॥
>
> Chapter 16 – verse 24

What is right and what is wrong needs endorsement from the scriptures. This is needed because impact of *Maya* (attraction to the material world) is so strong that one can easily come under its sway and get attracted to everything in this material world, which does not last for ever.

Once attracted to this material world, one can define the rules to win over it and that is where one goes wrong because that behaviour one may adopt may not have endorsement of the Lord as mentioned in the scriptures.

God is advising people to follow the scriptures in performing your duties. One who does not follow these and goes with his own set of rules can neither live happily, nor die peacefully nor reach the desired destination of God's home after leaving the body (death).

God decides whom to meet

> Hardly one among thousands of men strives to realise Me; of those striving Yogis, again, some rare one devoting himself exclusively to Me, knows Me in reality.
>
> हजारों मनुष्योंमें कोई एक मेरी प्राप्तिके लिये यत्न करता है और उन यत्न करनेवाले योगियोंमें भी कोई एक मेरे परायण होकर मुझको तत्त्वसे अर्थात् यथार्थरूपसे जानता है ॥
>
> Chapter 7 - verse 3

God decides whom he wants to meet. He meets the deserving individual through his own soul. One got to have a good reason on why he should meet us. In the past different deserving people had created different ways and reasons to meet God.

He meets one of the thousands of thousands who are sincere in their efforts to find him and with his blessings; they become successful in meeting God.

Out of thousand souls, only one soul becomes a pure devotee and among those devotees only a rare one loving soul knows him in Truth.

Many people worship throughout their life and many worship occasionally. Some people regularly chant God's name. Some are busy in doing social service and helping the needy, yet others are always busy working only for themselves. Some give part of their money to the more deserving, some do regular fasting. Some people have no time for these activities but perform all their natural duties religiously.

Question comes to the mind of those seeking God – Whom does God meet and how. The answer to this question is explained beautifully in one of the Upanishads (engraved in Birla Mandir, Kurukshetra).

"God does not meet people just by sharing money with the poor, or by reading too many scriptures or by doing excessive penance, etc. God meets one whom he wants to meet and he shows himself to the deserving person through the devotee's soul".

So, we need to have a reason in our life and in our behaviour that is compelling enough for God to meet us.

Many devotees in the past created reasons for Him to meet and they followed different paths like Sankhyayoga and *Karmayoga*.

Many Yogis are seated in *Himalayas, Badrinath* and *Rishikesh*. These Yogis have left everything in search of God and there is a saying that if you are sincere in your efforts to find God, you will find him.

One of the best books to be read about Yogis is the 'Autobiography of a *Yogi*' by Paramahansa Yogananda. It is a great proof of Lord's presence and existence and one can find great teachings in that book that confirm God's presence everywhere around us.

Meera found him through simple innocent love living outside her home. Gopis got him through simple and innocent love. *Prahlad* got him through simple love and devotion. They did not know Yoga methods but were great devotees, sincere and hungry lovers of God.

Meera belonged to King's family and had every possible material thing available to her. But she got so deeply in love with Lord Krishna that she left everything and spent all her life worshipping and remembering Lord Krishna. She was given a bowl of poison by the king. Knowing well that this is poison, she drank it remembering Lord Krishna and nothing happened to her. The idol of Krishna that Meera worshipped all her life is now kept in *Jagdeesh* Temple, Udaipur. She is an example of extreme love and devotion for Lord Krishna.

Arjuna, howsoever men seek Me, even so do I respond to them; for all men follow My path in everyway.

हे अर्जुन! जो भक्त मुझे जिस प्रकार भजते हैं, मैं भी उनको उसी प्रकार भजता हूँ; क्योंकि सभी मनुष्य सब प्रकारसे मेरे ही मार्गका अनुसरण करते हैं ॥

Chapter 4 - verse 11

Lord Krishna says, "All of them as they surrender unto Me I reward accordingly. Everyone follows My path in all respects, O son of *Partha*". When you love God and when you worship God, you actually follow his path only as he is the source of all inspiration. The way Meera worshipped Lord Krishna, same way Lord Krishna remembered and loved her all the time because the inspiration of love is drawn from him. He is the repository of love and emotions.

Krishna taught Arjun to reach him through the righteous war where millions of people lost their lives in a battle that lasted for 18 days. He reached God through performing his natural duties without attachment. This is called karmayoga. Bhagavad Gita teaches Karmyoga as the simplest, most promising and easiest way to reach him which is just performing your natural duties rightfully without expectation of any fruits and remembering him all the time.

Different people follow different paths. But one thing is common in all of them and that is purity. One needs to purify himself before starting the journey towards him; otherwise the journey itself will not begin even if one keeps trying throughout one's life.

A deserving person will listen about soul and God (Oversoul)

A deserving person is the one who has adopted the right *karmas* and has started purifying his inner self. He gets further support from God as he advances on his journey towards God.

Soul in every human being belongs to Oversoul (Some call him OM, some call him Krishna and many others see God in different forms).

Not everyone gets the desire to listen about soul. It is only a deserving person that takes interest and listens about the God and soul. One in thousands will have that desire and again one in thousands among them will follow God's defined path to *Liberation* and finally reach him.

> Hardly any great soul perceives this soul as marvelous, scarce another great soul likewise speaks thereof as marvelous, and scarce another worthy one hears of it as marvelous, while there are some who know it not even on hearing of it.
>
> कोई एक महापुरुष ही इस आत्माको आश्चर्यकी भाँति देखता है और वैसे ही दूसरा कोई महापुरुष ही इसके तत्त्वका आश्चर्यकी भाँति वर्णन करता है तथा दूसरा कोई अधिकारी पुरुष ही इसे आश्चर्यकी भाँति सुनता है और कोई-कोई तो सुनकर भी इसको नहीं जानता ॥
>
> Chapter 2 - verse 29

Lord says only an *Adhikari* person will listen about the soul. This means only those people who are on the path of purification and deserve to go up will listen about Bhagavad Gita and not everyone.

Bhagavad Gita is a very pure scripture, if understood and followed rightly can lead to liberation for sure within this birth. Similar teachings exist in different religions. However God's teachings attract only a deserving soul. A deserving soul has to be pure, others who do not deserve to go to his home will not get the opportunity to hear about the soul or even if they hear, then also they will not follow its teachings.

Lord says – I am spiritual science of the self (Soul)

Reading Bhagavad Gita and the other scriptures for one's upliftment is also the highest level of spiritual service to the lord. Bhagavad Gita is both - Lord and *Guru.*

Lord Krishna says that among sciences, I am the spiritual science of the self. Lord has identified himself to the Spiritual Science which means reading scriptures is indeed reading God himself.

> Arjuna, I am the beginning, the middle and the end of all creations. Of all knowledge, I am the knowledge of the soul (metaphysics); among disputants, I am the right type of discussion.
>
> हे अर्जुन! सृष्टियोंका आदि और अन्त तथा मध्य भी मैं ही हूँ। मैं विद्याओंमें अध्यात्मविद्या अर्थात् ब्रह्मविद्या और परस्पर विवाद करनेवालोंका तत्त्व-निर्णयके लिये किया जानेवाला वाद हूँ॥
>
> Chapter 10 – verse 32

Reading scriptures is a way of meditation that purifies your inner self and takes you closer to God. Lord has explained various forms in which he is present among us. Among sciences, he is present as spiritual science. Again those who are pure devotees and on journey of purification will get attracted towards the spiritual science and not everyone.

God lives above time

His home is where time does not change anything. His home is self illuminated where sunshine does not reach and devotees who go there do not return to this mortal world. Everything below his home is governed by time and will get destroyed with time sooner or later.

> Arjuna, all the worlds from Brahmaloka (the heavenly realm of the Creator, Brahma) downwards are liable to birth and rebirth. But, O son of *Kunti*, on attaining Me there is no rebirth (For, while I am beyond Time, regions like Brahmaloka, being conditioned by time, are transitory).
>
> हे अर्जुन! ब्रह्मलोकपर्यन्त सब लोक पुनरावर्ती हैं, परन्तु हे कुन्तीपुत्र! मुझको प्राप्त होकर पुनर्जन्म नहीं होता; क्योंकि मैं कालातीत हूँ और ये सब ब्रह्मादिके लोक कालके द्वारा सीमित होनेसे अनित्य हैं ॥
>
> Chapter 8 - verse 16

Lord Krishna says – I am *Kalaatit* which means that Lord is above time. Everything is controlled by the time. We are heading towards death every moment, journey is just for few years. Before we realise the real purpose of our life, we will be history. One day time will destroy each one of us. Sun will lose its shine after millions of years but even millions of years will go and its shine and energy is governed by time. Earth will get destroyed one day and that can also be measured by time. Time is the ruler for this material world.

However, there is one place that will never get destroyed, i.e. God's home beyond time. He controls time. Sunshine does not reach his place and his home is always illuminated. Some call him Krishna, some call him Rama. Some see the Goddess

Mahalaxmi and some worship the God as OM. Some feel his presence and worship him in the shape of a human being and some worship him as a name and some as an Oversoul without any shape.

Goddess Durga came over to earth at the age of six years and was worshipped in *Kaal Kandoli* for twelve years. At the end of this period, the Goddess was six years old only. Time was under the Goddess and could not make any changes in the Devi. *Vaishno Devi* is worshipped as a child and has been worshipped as a child for thousands of years. Time does not change the Goddess as Goddess is above time. Gods appear on earth to help the devotees and to keep the righteousness in order and go back to their home (above time) after completing the purpose of their appearance on earth.

Mata Durga

Sometimes God appears on earth instantly without taking birth and sometime God follows the birth cycle. This does not mean anything other than his own decision on his way to carry out his own set of wishes for human welfare and to run this earth. Devotee's love makes God appear instantly.

Neither the sun nor the moon nor fire can illumine that supreme self – effulgent state, attaining which they never return to this world; that is my supreme abode.

जिस परमपदको प्राप्त होकर मनुष्य लौटकर संसारमें नहीं आते, उस स्वयंप्रकाश परमपदको न सूर्य प्रकाशित कर सकता है, न चन्द्रमा और न अग्नि ही; वही मेरा परमधाम है ॥

Chapter 15 - verse 6

Paramdham or Final Destination is God's home. His Home is away from this world, it is self illumined. Once you reach God's home, then you are above the basic time lines followed by the world. Reaching his home is called liberation. You still work there as God is always working but you are beyond all the sufferings of birth, old age, death and worldly pains, etc. There is no influence of material world there, no feelings of hatred and jealousy. There are no sufferings. That is a beautiful destination to aim for. We have limited time and we should not spend a fraction of our time in doing any act that does not take us closer to his home.

There is a lot of attraction in Maya as this is also His creation, we need to overcome that attraction and the only way to overcome that attraction is to get his blessings and his blessings will come only with *Jaap*.

Soul that keeps us alive belongs to God (Oversoul)

Soul in every one of us belongs to Oversoul. Soul is complete God. It provides energy and light required to the body to stay alive. Once soul departs from the body to go to another body, this body cannot function despite all efforts. An individual's identity in God's eyes is soul not the body. Soul with cosmic energy helps us to talk, listen, eat, smell, think, decide, etc. Once the soul departs, body cannot perform these functions, as their collective consciousness is the soul.

Just as boyhood, youth and old age are attributed to the soul through this body, even so it attains another body. The wise man does not get deluded about this.

जैसे जीवात्माकी इस देहमें बालकपन, जवानी और वृद्धावस्था होती है, वैसे ही अन्य शरीरकी प्राप्ति होती है; उस विषयमें धीर पुरुष मोहित नहीं होता ॥

Chapter 2 – verse 13

After death, soul migrates to the new body. If the identity is body, then it will be lost very soon. Our self identity is soul which belongs to the Oversoul. Soul migrates to the new body as per the nature and karmas of the person.

If karmas are bad and nature is full of ego and anger, human birth may not be the next destination; it may be an animal or an insect. All these births are lower world births. If the karmas are good and nature is good, next birth may be a good human life or may migrate to the higher worlds of *Devtas*.

Soul is presence of God in you. It is ignorance that one does not feel the presence. People with pious eyes can see this truth. When this truth is realised, then God is known to the individual.

Since soul is complete God, its home is above time. Sooner or later, it is going to get there. Since it lives above time it will never get destroyed so you will always be alive in one form or the other.

Your true identity is your soul and soul never dies

Your identity is soul and you will always be alive. Your soul is complete God and hence you should never do the acts that God does not like or approve. Soul records all your karmas.

> The soul is never born, nor it ever dies; nor does it become after being born. For, it is unborn, eternal, everlasting and primeval; even though the body is slain, the soul is not.
>
> यह आत्मा किसी कालमें भी न तो जन्मता है और न मरता ही है तथा न यह उत्पन्न होकर फिर होनेवाला ही है; क्योंकि यह अजन्मा, नित्य, सनातन और पुरातन है; शरीरके मारे जानेपर भी यह नहीं मारा जाता ॥
>
> Chapter 2 - verse 20

> This soul is un-manifest; it is incomprehensible and it is spoken of as immutable. Therefore, knowing it as such, you should not grieve.
>
> यह आत्मा अव्यक्त है, यह आत्मा अचिन्त्य है और यह आत्मा विकाररहित कहा जाता है। इससे हे अर्जुन! इस आत्माको उपर्युक्त प्रकारसे जानकर तू शोक करनेको योग्य नहीं है अर्थात् तुझे शोक करना उचित नहीं है ॥
>
> Chapter 2- verse 25

Ram Sharnam is a religious organisation, their Guruji (Satyanand ji Maharaj) who founded this institute meditated on God for a very long time. Finally, Guru ji went to *Dalhousie* and sat quietly in a room for many days. One day, Guruji heard "Ram *Bhaj*, Ram Bhaj" repeatedly. When God wanted to meet him, Guru only heard God's voice. Guruji requested God for *Darshan*. God's voice asked Guruji 'In which form do you want to see me'. Guruji said, "I do not know your form, so please appear in the form that you feel is right for me to see you".

Then Guruji saw the environment illumined and राम name appeared. Guruji started *Ram Sharnam* which has thousands of followers today. Followers of Ram Sharnam meditate on राम. *Amritvani* is sung in many places everyday by the devotees.

राम राम   राम राम   राम राम   राम राम   राम राम   राम राम

राम राम   राम राम   राम राम   राम राम   राम राम   राम राम

> Lord says: Among purifiers, I am the wind; among wielders of arms, I am Sri Rama. Among fishes, I am the shark; and among streams, I am the Ganges.
>
> मैं पवित्र करनेवालोंमें वायु और शस्त्रधारियोंमें श्रीराम हूँ तथा मछलियोंमें मगर हूँ और नदियोंमें श्रीभागीरथी गंगाजी हूँ॥
>
> Chapter 10 – verse 31

Lord Rama was also Krishna/Vishnu's incarnation – The Supreme Power as we all know that God is only one. We should feel His presence everywhere.

> Lord says: Arjuna, I am the universal Self seated in the hearts of all beings: so, I alone am the beginning, the middle and also the end of all beings.
>
> हे अर्जुन! जिस प्रकार एक ही सूर्य इस सम्पूर्ण ब्रह्माण्डको प्रकाशित करता है, उसी प्रकार एक ही आत्मा सम्पूर्ण क्षेत्रको प्रकाशित करता है॥
>
> Chapter 10 – verse20

In the verse above, God has clearly stated that God himself is our soul in every individual, i.e. yourself, your friends, your neighbours, your relatives, in those who are unknown to you and the ones whom you do not like. It is the same God present in everyone.

This knowledge changes the vision of the learned people – People whose intelligence is strongly connected with their mind understand the presence of God in everyone hence they do not hate anyone.

Soul remains pure even if karmas are not pure

Soul never gets contaminated. It is God's presence in the individuals irrespective of the body – be it human beings, devtas or animals. It is a witness to everything you do. It decides your destiny for the next birth based on your nature and karmas in your present birth.

Soul always stays pure and untouched. It provides the energy to the body to stay alive and perform karmas. It is the carrier of your karmas to the next life. It is a witness of all your karmas. It never gets impure even if your karmas are not pure.

It is a complete God in every individual. It carries intelligence and mind to the next destination according to one's karmas. It provides light and energy to the body like Sun provides light and energy to the universe. Soul's departure from the body leaves it dead ready for cremation.

Lord says : Arjuna , as the one sun illumines this entire universe , so the one Atma (Spirit) illumines the whole Kshetra (Field)

हे अर्जुन! जिस प्रकार एक ही सूर्य इस सम्पूर्ण ब्रह्माण्डको प्रकाशित करता है, उसी प्रकार एक ही आत्मा सम्पूर्ण क्षेत्रको प्रकाशित करता है॥

Chapter 13 – verse 33

Lord further says: As the all pervading ether is not contaminated by reason of its subtlety, though permeating the body, the Self is not affected by the attributes of the body due to Its attributeless character.

जिस प्रकार सर्वत्र व्याप्त आकाश सूक्ष्म होनेके कारण लिप्त नहीं होता, वैसे ही देहमें सर्वत्र स्थित आत्मा निर्गुण होनेके कारण देहके गुणोंसे लिप्त नहीं होता॥

Chapter 13 – verse 32

Soul inside us is always connected to God

Our soul constantly draws energy from the Oversoul. Soul's ultimate home is Oversoul. Guru can reveal all these truths when we approach him with a pure and humble heart. Bhagavad Gita is also a Guru for a devotee.

Human birth in itself is one of the greatest wonders of God. We are alive and this is the greatest wonders of the lord. Our soul draws energy from somewhere but we are just not able to realise it. It is always connected with the Oversoul which is beyond Time. So soul in us belongs to the Oversoul, that is home of the soul, that is why Lord Krishna said that this soul will never get destroyed.

The eternal *Jivatma* in this body is a fragment of My own self; and it is that alone which draws around itself the mind and the five senses, which abide in Prakrti.

इस देहमें यह सनातन जीवात्मा मेरा ही अंश है और वही इन प्रकृतिमें स्थित मन और पाँचों इन्द्रियोंको आकर्षण करता है ॥

Chapter 15 - verse 7

Soul is in constant dialogue with the Oversoul, while we do not know about it. Soul monitors our karmas, keeps a stock of it and is still always pure and untouched. Many people constantly reach out to the soul through meditation and Yoga and these people know about the presence of soul and God inside. These people when reached can be the guide to other deserving human beings. It is only a deserving person that will look for these God realised souls and take shelter in their guidance.

Lord says: Understand the true nature of that knowledge by approaching seers of Truth. If you prostrate at their feet, render them service, and question them with an open and guileless heart, those wise seers of Truth will instruct you in that Knowledge.

उस ज्ञानको तू तत्त्वदर्शी ज्ञानियोंके पास जाकर समझ, उनको भलीभाँति दण्डवत्-प्रणाम करनेसे, उनकी सेवा करनेसे और कपट छोड़कर सरलतापूर्वक प्रश्न करनेसे वे परमात्मतत्त्वको भलीभाँति जाननेवाले ज्ञानी महात्मा तुझे उस तत्त्वज्ञानका उपदेश करेंगे ॥

Chapter 4 - verse 34

According to Bhagavad Gita, a Guru is the one who is seer of the Truth and one who can impart that knowledge to the deserving ones. Such people are difficult to find if your inner self is not pure. Once the inner self is purified, God's system will bring these people in contact with you. Bhagavad Gita can also work like a Guru since it came from Krishna and there cannot be any teacher greater than God Himself. God said that among the sciences, I am the science of the soul. So reading Bhagavad Gita is reading Krishna Himself.

However journey to God's home will start only after the internal purification.

God is creator of love and He loves you more than you do

Story of Vrinda's love and Krishna's surrender to Vrinda's love.

Vrinda became *Tulsi* plant. Also a proof that whole system of universe runs with Lord's energy. Out of immense love for Tulsi, Lord allowed Himself to be cursed and become a *Saligrama*.

Tulsi is worshipped in all temples and Hindu homes. Tulsi's original name in human form was Vrinda. Vrindavan is named after Tulsi/Vrinda. When we offer food to Lord Krishna, a tulsi leaf is put on top of the food. Where tulsi is worshipped, no evil can happen. Krishna was married to Tulsi and this union is celebrated every year.

Vrinda idol in human form and Tulsi form

Vrinda wanted to reach Krishna as His loving devotee. Vrinda was known for her purity. Purity and love for Krishna made her very powerful even when she neither knew about her power nor wanted to use her power for any purpose. She once cursed Krishna when He came to her in a form where she could not recognise the Lord.

With the curse of Vrinda, Lord Krishna allowed Himself to become a stone and today Krishna is worshipped as Saligrama.

As soon as Krishna became a stone, there was restlessness in the entire universe (stars, human beings, devtas and animals). No one knew what happened to them till Tulsi freed up Krishna from the curse.

Vrinda had the power because of Krishna's blessings. Lord has immense love for his devotees. Lord is extremely loving by heart and love can bring Him down to the devotee. Krishna allowed Himself to be cursed and that shows how much He can love His devotees.

Celebrating that moment of love between Saligrama and Tulsi – a marriage is performed by Hindus every year.

Connect intelligence and mind (through meditation) to reach the soul

Intelligence connected with mind can help realise the presence of the soul inside. Through soul, one can see and reach the Oversoul as soul belongs to Oversoul. If intelligence does not connect with mind, then individual can never become a God realised soul despite all attempts and activities.

Some people are very intelligent and very logical and can do excellent analysis of any script or writing. What comes in as a hindrance for them to realise the God?

Bhagavad Gita has an answer to this question. It is connection of intelligence with the mind. Intelligent person may have a very good interlock between intelligence and mind or may have no connection between the two. In either case, a person may be highly successful in his field or career but one whose intelligence is connected with the mind may be much closer to the Lord than the other one.

Suppose, someone tells us that you will die one day. Intelligence knows this for years and it may react back that this is no new news. It may even bring in anger in the person for such a well known message getting repeated. However for a God realised soul, it is a new message every day. He realises that another day is gone from his life. It will bring in feelings of being helpful to other people and being nicer to others in this world. He creates an environment of love and not hatred. He creates an environment to help people and not punish. He wants to share part of his wealth with more deserving people. He becomes more humble.

Soul is most powerful. But soul can be reached only by intelligence connected with the mind. At the time of death, soul takes away the intelligence and mind from the person and the body is left behind. So, if your intelligence is negative as you have been using it for wrong purposes, then in your next birth, you will be born with the same intelligence and same negativity. If you have a positive and a helpful attitude and you are not a harmful person, you will have the same positive qualities in your next birth.

Now this is further clubbed with your karmas in life. If one has a negative thinking, then quite likely, his karmas will also be negative. If one's karmas are negative, then he falls down from his current status which means that a very rich person may get to miseries in his next birth or may even go to the lower births which is the births of animals and other species, so he may end up losing his human life in the next birth.

One needs to be very conscious of his karmas and use of his intelligence and behaviour. Human birth is a very short life but has long implications that a person with wrong deeds for few years may end up paying it back with millions of years in lower lives and may still never be able to get out of it because lower one sinks, more the possibility that he will sink down further. Why? Because one sank down due to bad karmas and these bad karmas were earned due to negativity.

Bad karmas will sink the person and negativity will flow down with him to the next birth. With negativity in legacy and a tendency to do bad karmas and now with a harder environment because of bad karmas, that person in all likelihood is going to sink further because in tougher environment, he will adopt further negativity and do more bad karmas and this will eventually lead him to hell or lower worlds. Bad karmas make the environment in next birth harsher than this birth, this may get into a vicious circle and one may end up in the lower world of animals and insects.

So, one should be making constant efforts to uplift oneself in the eyes of God by always doing good karmas and with intelligence well used for his people's benefit and not to harm the world.

Lord said: The mind is restless no doubt, and difficult to curb, Arjuna; but it can be brought under control by repeated practice (of meditation) and by the exercise of dispassion, O son of Kunti.

श्रीभगवान् बोले—हे महाबाहो! नि:सन्देह मन चञ्चल और कठिनतासे वशमें होनेवाला है; परन्तु हे कुन्तीपुत्र अर्जुन! यह अभ्यास और वैराग्यसे वशमें होता है॥

Chapter 6 - verse 35

Lord says: Yoga is difficult of achievement by one whose mind is not subdued by him; however, who has the mind under control, and is ceaselessly striving, it can be easily attained through practice. Such is My conviction.

जिसका मन वशमें किया हुआ नहीं है, ऐसे पुरुषद्वारा योग दुष्प्राप्य है और वशमें किये हुए मनवाले प्रयत्नशील पुरुषद्वारा साधनसे उसका प्राप्त होना सहज है—यह मेरा मत है॥

Chapter 6 - verse 36

Intelligence and mind will not connect for a material engrossed person

If the binding between intelligence and mind is weak, one can never realise the presence of soul. This means the person acts according to his own whims and is not a God realised soul. He is ignorant on what is right and what is wrong in the spiritual system, he may be very intelligent in the material world and the material system has been set up by none other than human beings.

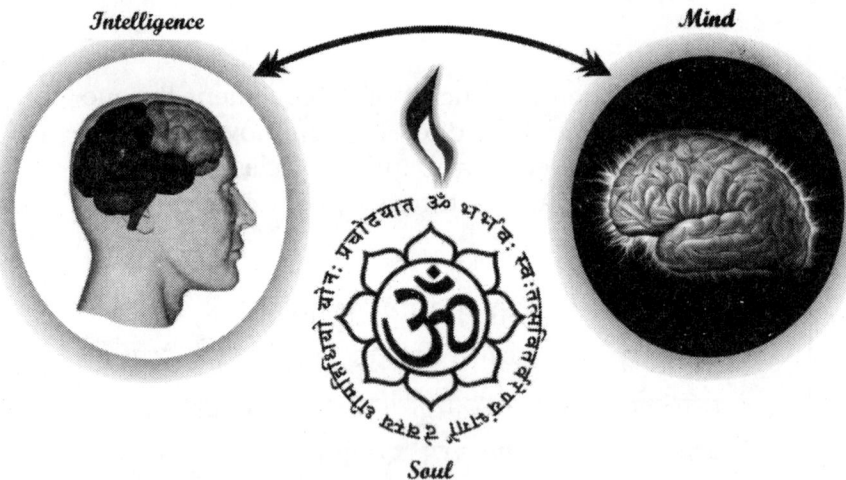

This person has no realisation that there is a soul within his body.

A person whose mind is not connected with intelligence

- *Is focussed on material gains even if he needs to adopt some unfair means.*
- *Does not share his wealth with the poor and needy.*
- *Does not mind hurting sentiments of the people at home and in place of work.*
- *Is jealous, angry, egoistic and always full of material desires.*
- *Can't feel the pain of a crying child or the suffering of a human being.*

Intelligence and mind will connect for a God realised soul
(Through meditation)

If the binding between intelligence and mind is strong, then soul is well within the reach of that person. Intelligence and mind consult each other for every action and they evaluate the results of the action in the spiritual system, not in the material system.

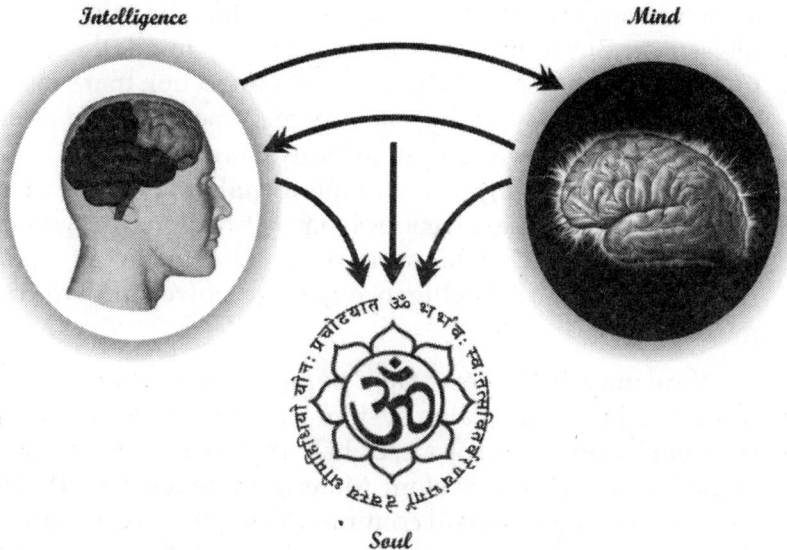

This person's behaviour will show that he is a God realised soul.

(He achieves all this with meditation)

- *He does not hurt people, nor does he get hurt by anyone.*
- *He is careful on not adopting any unfair means for earning his livelihood.*
- *Not attracted to the material world even while he lives in that world.*
- *Shares his money with the poor and needy.*
- *Can feel the pain of a crying child or a poor heart.*
- *Has controlled Anger - Ego - Desire.*

Intelligence and meditation help control the wandering mind

When intelligence and mind are connected and intelligence controls the mind, karmas become purified and soul reveals its presence to that purified individual.

One is always attracted towards many material things in the world. This is called *Maya*. Some get attracted towards money, some towards power, some towards enmity, and some towards wrong food and so on. This attraction is by the senses. But if one starts listening to the mind, then one finds that mind does not agree to every attraction that senses have. When we say, it does not agree, it means that it does not agree in God's value system. Now if one evaluates every attraction with intelligence and mind well interlocked, then one will find that one can control many attractions that got no recognition in God's value system. Mind has to be controlled by intelligence and intelligence is more powerful than the mind.

You may be a very rich person but money is not recognised in God's value system – another person who is poor but has integrity, peace, right karmas may be a very rich person in God's value system. Material system will end with death – God's system will continue. You will have a sudden discontinuity of all the material world in a split of a second, after death – nothing is yours in this material world even if you earned it with all your hard work and intelligence – now His system starts and rewards you for the future based on your karmas and not based on your material richness.

So, one should always connect intelligence with the mind. Do the right things as per God's system and make the journey beautiful after death. If one does not get worried about the life after death – this is ignorance and ignorance is Tamasika. So, one must change the rules of this game that one has defined for himself and instead follow the rules advised by the scriptures.

Lord said: The senses are said to be greater than the body; but greater than the senses is the mind. Greater than the mind is the intellect; and what is greater than the intellect is He, the self.

इन्द्रियोंको स्थूल शरीरसे पर यानी श्रेष्ठ, बलवान् और सूक्ष्म कहते हैं; इन इन्द्रियोंसे पर मन है, मनसे भी पर बुद्धि है और जो बुद्धिसे भी अत्यन्त पर है वह आत्मा है॥

Chapter 3 – verse 42

Thus, Arjuna, knowing the self which is higher than the intellect and subduing the mind by reason, kill this enemy in the form of desire that is hard to overcome.

इस प्रकार बुद्धिसे पर अर्थात् सूक्ष्म, बलवान् और अत्यन्त श्रेष्ठ आत्माको जानकर और बुद्धिके द्वारा मनको वशमें करके हे महाबाहो! तू इस कामरूप दुर्जय शत्रुको मार डाल॥

Chapter 3 – verse 43

Source : *www.bhagavad-gita.us*

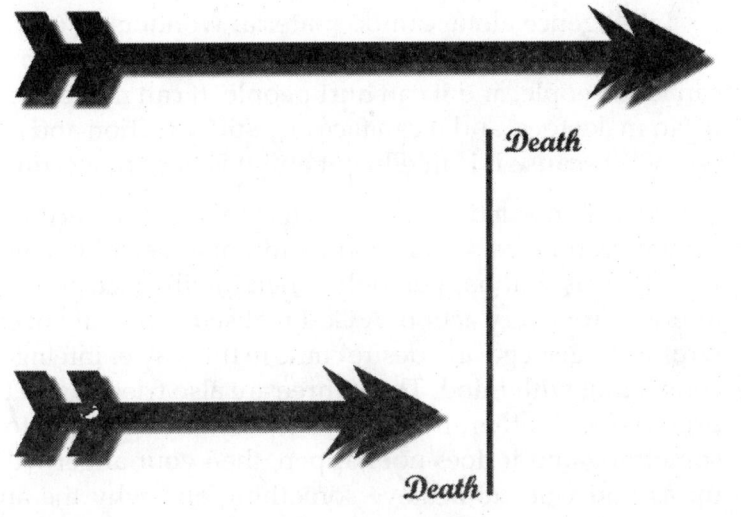

Anger – Ego – Desire are three gates to hell

Why intelligence is not connected with Mind? Because Anger, Ego, Desire comes in the way. Degree of their strength varies from person to person. Stronger the three, more away are you from the God irrespective of your social status and material kingdom. If these are not worked upon and left loose, they will just keep growing stronger and can take one to the lower world.

Intelligence alone can do material wonders. It can earn money, it can discover new things, it can do inventions, it can love people, and it can hurt people. It can make friends, it can make foes, and it can face any stiff situation and come out of it because it is intelligent and it is very powerful.

What is needed is to channelise this intelligence in the right direction (as seen by God and not as seen by material world). This will happen only when intelligence and mind interlock for every action. A God realised soul will never go wrong. Anger, ego and desire come in the way of intelligence connecting with mind. These three are also friends and they promote each other. If you have a very strong desire to get something and it does not happen, then your anger will go up as you want to achieve something and why the anger goes up, it is because of the ego. Ego does not tolerate that this can happen to you.

For a minute, if one realises one's position, then one can start working on the Ego. Sun will keep shining without you, earth will keep moving without you, world will keep going without you. Everything was working before you came on the earth and everything will keep going as it is when you depart. Currency, position, status, titles is this entire world's creation. It is not recognised by Him. He recognises nature, karmas, soul, intelligence and mind, your behaviour to His creation.

Lord is the only leader. He was the only leader and He will be the only Leader. Many leaders created by this earth have come and gone. He is the only one who stays. You need to take shelter under Lord for liberation. He is the only one who can take you out of this pain of birth and death, pain of old age, pain of sufferings. He is the only one worth taking shelter under. Sooner you realise this, you will be freed from this bondage. All religions follow their leaders and they all emerge from the same source, same God in different forms.

And remember, this journey to Him is not short. He is inviting you to come to Him by giving this human body to you, but it is not so easy to reach Him. It is important to start the journey towards Him, then you know you will cover this journey in few births if not in one birth and actually it may not happen in one birth.

Many have tried. You need to commit and start moving towards him and the best thing to happen will be that you will get his support for this journey. If He truly loves you, then He will answer all your prayers and demands that help you move closer to him. He may not answer or recognise your demands that are short lived or their shine will impact your vision and may not take you closer to Him. At this time, determination to start the journey is important. He will support you unconditionally.

Section 2

Heaven is not on the way to God's home

Shiv – Parvati

The consciousness of a God realised soul is different than a materially engrossed person

When you follow His path with love and devotion, He will help you reach Him. Stronger you follow the pull of material world; more you will keep going away from Him.

Material world means everything that leads to sense enjoyment. Money, power, material richness, body comforts more than needed. There is a lot of attraction in this for the people who are highly awakened in the material system. Spiritual world means sacrifice, i.e. doing your duties, meditating, helping the needy ones, feeling the pain of others and through all this uplifting yourself towards God.

If one is a God realised soul, then he does not see his belongingness to the material world even while one is living in the material world. He does not enjoy it with his senses but just sees everything as a blessing of God and goes into renunciation.

As one starts withdrawing his belongingness to material world and does not feel envious and gets rid of anger and ego, then one starts getting the pull from the spiritual system of God.

As an example when you need to leave the gravity of the earth, first you need to work hard and get yourself out of the gravity. In a similar way, you need to work hard to get rid of the material attraction and false sense by having a complete control on your senses, then you will get the pull from the Oversoul.

When you are out of the gravity of material world, the pull of spiritual system will start working on you.

Heaven is not on way to God's home

For a God realised soul wanting liberation and to reach God's home – heaven cannot be the destination. For a God realised soul - destination is Lord Krishna (Way to God's home does not pass through heaven. Heaven does not mean that your next destination is God's home). If you think that way, it means you have not understood His rules for the game. He decides your next birth based on your karmas.

> Lord says: Arjuna, those who are full of worldly desires and devoted to the letter of the *Vedas*, who look upon heaven as the supreme goal and argue that there is nothing beyond heaven, are unwise. They utter flowery speech recommending many rituals of various kinds for the attainment of pleasure and power with rebirth as their fruit. Those whose minds are carried away by such words, and who are deeply attached to pleasures and worldly power, cannot attain the determinate intellect concentrated on God.
>
> हे अर्जुन! जो भोगोंमें तन्मय हो रहे हैं, जो कर्मफलके प्रशंसक वेदवाक्योंमें ही प्रीति रखते हैं, जिनकी बुद्धिमें स्वर्ग ही परम प्राप्य वस्तु है और जो स्वर्गसे बढ़कर दूसरी कोई वस्तु ही नहीं है—ऐसा कहनेवाले हैं, वे अविवेकीजन इस प्रकारकी जिस पुष्पित अर्थात् दिखाऊ शोभायुक्त वाणीको कहा करते हैं जो कि जन्मरूप कर्मफल देनेवाली एवं भोग तथा ऐश्वर्यकी प्राप्तिके लिये नाना प्रकारकी बहुत-सी क्रियाओंका वर्णन करनेवाली है, उस वाणीद्वारा जिनका चित्त हर लिया गया है, जो भोग और ऐश्वर्यमें अत्यन्त आसक्त हैं; उन पुरुषोंकी परमात्मामें निश्चयात्मिका बुद्धि नहीं होती॥
>
> Chapter 2- verse 42-43-44

People define their own rules for the game of this life. Some people define getting huge money a win; some define huge power as win. These rules are your own defined rules and not His rules. He monitors the process of birth and death so his rules matter; your rules do not matter in his system. Your rules matter only in this material world.

People and their actions are driven by ego, anger and desire. When you work for yourself and your family (and not God's family) but do good karmas, do regular visits to temples, help the poor and are also strongly driven by your own set of rules where desire and anger touch you in every moment of this birth, one can reach heaven. Heaven is nothing but a reward of your good deeds, recognition of good deeds like you reward people with material things when they produce good business results. Scriptures also have various activities defined that if those are performed, they lead you to heaven after death like many *yagyas* and *havans*, feeding others on auspicious days, etc. All these are definitely good deeds with no doubt and are needed for one's upliftment. But there is more needed if one wants to bypass the way to heaven and go to God's home.

Heaven is a much better place to be in after death than hell. But heaven is not God's home. Heaven is no way end of your sufferings. It is a temporary shelter in a cool, good place. Heaven no way means that your next destination is God's home.

What is heaven? After death, the soul migrates to the *astral world*. If one has been performing good deeds in his current birth but not ready for God's home, he lives innumerable number of years in a place that is gifted with all sorts of pleasures. No new karmas are performed. After enjoyment for number of years when the fruits of their merits is exhausted, they fall back on the earth in a good and rich family. People with divine vision see this as a sheer waste of time with negative returns, why negative returns because it burns both – Time and merits of your good deeds for enjoyment.

So, Krishna wanted God realised souls to be very watchful of their deeds. Are they following those parts of the scriptures that are teaching their way to heaven? These are after all scriptures and they got to guide you on what to do and what not to do. But following the activities wherein the result is lots of material things on earth and heaven after death is not for the people who are looking for reaching God's home.

God has created everything and needs all the creatures, be it devtas up in the higher worlds or human beings or creatures of the lower worlds like animals. You can define any of these as your next destination after this birth and start working accordingly. He needs all of them, he is giving shelter to all of them. But he is teaching you to always lift yourself up. What is meant by lifting yourself up is starting the journey towards God and one who is seeing the destination as God, cannot engage in activities that end him up in heaven.

Any place below time is going to get destroyed at some point of time. This includes heaven. Going to heaven is making all enjoyments and not performing new karma. Going to heaven cannot lead to liberation. Your destination needs to be the *Parbrahm* which is God's place where time does not make any changes, is all peace and is self illumined. That is the highest level of enjoyment which is ever lasting.

> Lord says: Having enjoyed the extensive heaven-world, they return to this world of mortals on the stock of their merits being exhausted. Thus devoted to the ritual with interested motive, recommended by the three Vedas as the means of attaining heavenly bliss, and seeking worldly enjoyments, they repeatedly come and go (i.e. ascend to heaven by virtue of their merits and return to earth when their fruit has been enjoyed).
>
> वे उस विशाल स्वर्गलोकको भोगकर पुण्य क्षीण होनेपर मृत्युलोकको प्राप्त होते हैं। इस प्रकार स्वर्गके साधनरूप तीनों वेदोंमें कहे हुए सकामकर्मका आश्रय लेनेवाले और भोगोंकी कामनावाले पुरुष बार-बार आवागमनको प्राप्त होते हैं, अर्थात् पुण्यके प्रभावसे स्वर्गमें जाते हैं और पुण्य क्षीण होनेपर मृत्युलोकमें आते हैं॥
>
> Chapter 9 verse 21

For a God realised soul, heaven is a sheer waste of time given by God to him. Hence your aspired destination should never be heaven. You may end up getting there because you fell short in your karmas for liberation but heaven should not be the aim.

If you perform good duties with attachment, you will end up in heaven for many years. Once you exhaust your account of good deeds, you will fall back on earth in a good environment. The way of life should not be this up and down journey between heaven and earth. There is no path which goes to God's home from heaven but you need to come back on earth. The path to God's home is from earth directly.

Going to heaven, higher worlds after death brings you back to earth as humans after merits are exhausted. Migration to God's home is liberation and there is no return from it.

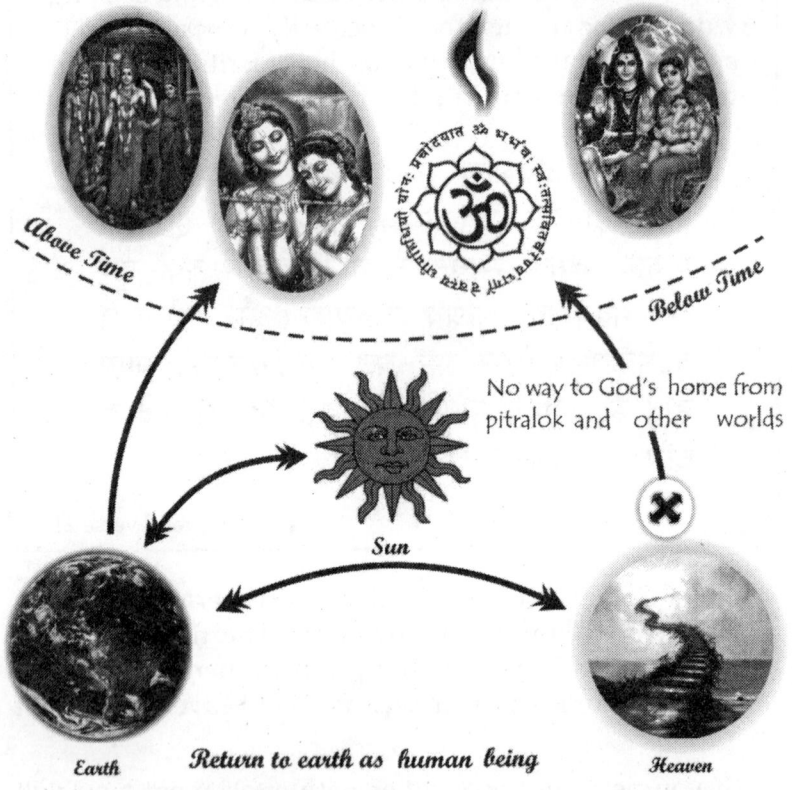

Migration to higher worlds after death brings you back to human world - same pain of birth, death and old age again.

God does not decide your actions, nature influences actions

God does not decide one's actions or karmas for any life. It is left on one's individual decision on what one wants to do. But one's nature that includes intelligence, mind, anger, ego, desire, likings and dislikings that one carried forward from his last birth (which is cumulative of many previous births) acts so strong on an individual that anything about one's behaviour can be predicted.

Your birth in an individual family, country, riches, intellect is not incidental. It is the result of previous karmas. You will again get all this in the next birth is not certain.

> Lord says : God determines neither the doership nor the doings of men, nor even their contact with the fruit of actions ; but it is Nature alone that does all this.
>
> परमेश्वर मनुष्योंके न तो कर्तापनकी, न कर्मोंकी और न कर्मफलके संयोगकी ही रचना करते हैं; किन्तु स्वभाव ही बर्त रहा है॥
>
> Chapter 5 - verse 14

God does not write or define your set of karmas but still God knows how everyone of us is going to behave. Pandits and astrologers write your birth chart and based on the birth chart, they do all possible calculations and predictions and if your birth chart has been written accurately and the person analysing your birth chart is highly learned, then he can very accurately predict almost everything about you. Now God has not defined your karmas but people who know how to read the birth chart can accurately predict. This is true that they can predict. Position of stars at the time of birth is a reflection of one's nature and karmas from the previous birth and position of these stars influence your behaviour through your life and that is the prediction. Not written by God but written by your own karmas.

Your birth at a particular time, in a particular family and in a particular country is not incidental. You earn all these things based on your previous karmas. If you were an intelligent person in your previous birth, so will you be in this birth and one can predict this from the birth chart. If you lived the life of an angry person previously, you will be an angry person by birth and learned people can analyse this from your birth chart. Support of stars at the time of your birth is positioned as per your karmas and as per your nature. If you are born in a rich family and you become the owner of wealth by birth, this is earned from your previous karmas, this is not incidental.

If you are born in a family that has all sorts of conflicts, it is again an earning you got from your previous karmas.

Now you have following major influences on you when you are born

- Your Nature, i.e. Feelings of anger – ego – desire – jealousy, etc.
- Your Environment – family, richness, influence of environment.
- Your state of meditation and attraction towards God – you start from where you have left in your last birth.

These collectively determine your behaviour. Thousands of people just get driven by these influences and work accordingly. One in thousands (the blessed one) decides not to get attracted to all these riches and gets more attracted towards God and starts working hard on this journey. Also one in thousands who was a God realised soul in previous birth will get attracted more towards the material things in course of life and may move away from God and start falling down in the spiritual journey and start moving forward in the material journey.

Key is whether we want to be driven by our nature or we want to drive it. If you want to be driven, the journey is easy – just go with the flow of the water and you will keep going in the material world – deeper and deeper. If you want to select your destination towards God's home, then there is a task ahead.

You need to start the journey towards his home and when that home is so beautiful then journey cannot be less beautiful. It is a change of attitude and that change is for the good. Going away from material attraction may feel painful but that is for the nectar that one is shortly going to enjoy following the journey towards God. You can enjoy so much in the journey that you may get least worried on whether you will reach God's home within one birth or not.

Your love towards Him will get reciprocated very fast because you are a loving being. God, who has created love, knows how to love you much more than you do. His love is selfless and will make this journey so beautiful that you will wish that this journey never ends and when it ends, it ends at his home.

> Lord says: Now hear from Me the threefold joy too. That in which the striver finds enjoyment through practice of adoration, meditation and service to God etc. and whereby he reaches the end of sorrow – such a joy, though appearing as poison in the beginning, tastes like nectar in the end; hence that joy, born as it is of the placidity of mind brought about by meditation on God, has been declared as *Sattvika*.
>
> हे भरतश्रेष्ठ! अब तीन प्रकारके सुखको भी तू मुझसे सुन। जिस सुखमें साधक मनुष्य भजन, ध्यान और सेवादिके अभ्याससे रमण करता है और जिससे दुःखोंके अन्तको प्राप्त हो जाता है—जो ऐसा सुख है, वह आरम्भकालमें यद्यपि विषके तुल्य प्रतीत होता है, परन्तु परिणाममें अमृतके तुल्य है; इसलिये वह परमात्मविषयक बुद्धिके प्रसादसे उत्पन्न होनेवाला सुख सात्त्विक कहा गया है॥
>
> Chapter 18 - verse 36-37

Bhagavad Gita teaches you the way upward towards God's home. Just follow one of the teachings of Bhagavad Gita that does best to you in your current environment and state of the mind and it may change all your future during the rest of this life and after death.

Human birth is very short. Bad karmas for few years may get you to the lower worlds for millions of years. Good karmas for few years may take you to His home and liberate you from the birth-death cycle forever. This time cannot be ignored and let go without conscious thinking and working upon properly.

As you sow, so shall you reap

Good karmas will take you up; bad karmas will make you fall. Once you fall in one birth, there is a greater chance that you will fall further in the next birth because you will get a less friendly environment in your next birth if karmas are not good. Once you rise in one birth due to good karmas, there is a greater chance that you will further rise in next birth. It is a trend that will take you to God's home on one way and to animal life on the other way.

Accept your current environment which is your earning based on your previous karmas and move upwards.

> Lord said: This body, Arjuna is termed as the Field (Kshetra) and he who knows it, is called the knower of the Field (Ksetrajna) by the sages discerning the truth about both.
>
> जैसे खेतमें बोये हुए बीजोंका उनके अनुरूप फल समयपर प्रकट होता है, वैसे ही इसमें बोये हुए कर्मोंके संस्काररूप बीजोंका फल समयपर प्रकट होता है, इसलिये इसका नाम 'क्षेत्र' ऐसा कहा है।
>
> Chapter 13 – verse 1

This body has been compared with field. Like when you sow some seeds in the field, you reap the fruits in due course of time. Same way, whatever karma you perform with this body (good, bad and mixed), you reap the fruits of your karmas in due course of time which may partially be in this birth and more over a number of births. You keep accumulating the karmas and keep reaping the fruits of your karmas spread over many births. The soul in the body is witness to whatever you have been doing in various births and is complete God in you but never gets contaminated. It gives the power for the body to survive and it carries the karmas to the next birth.

If the next birth is that of animal or insect or other lower worlds, then no new karmas are allowed. This is just a suffering life for a defined period. On the opposite side, even in heaven, you perform no new karmas; it is just a reward and enjoyment for the defined period. Both in a way cannot be the desired destinations for God realised souls. Your journey and performance of new karmas starts from this birth with your current environment. Now you have to excel in this environment. You need to continue your journey towards God in this new environment.

There are chances that you will progress further and there are chances that you will go backwards. Environment can have an influence on you and you may decide to get driven by it or you may decide to drive the environment and make it friendlier for your journey forward.

Your nature from previous births and your environment earned based on your karmas are known to God. Major milestones of your life are pre-written where you have no or little control, these are called devas or self written compelling destiny but rest of it can be modified and changed by you by doing new good karmas. Even the destiny can be changed with very high sacrifice and devotion to God. That is the wonder of this human birth if one realises the value. But if one does not realise the value, then it will be gone for nothing.

Even intelligent men have little or no control on their nature

Nature drives you more than you drive the nature. That is the difference between an ordinary human being and a God realised soul who controls his nature.

> Lord says : All living creatures follow their tendencies; even the wise man acts according to the tendencies of his own nature. Of what use is restraint by force.
>
> सभी प्राणी प्रकृतिको प्राप्त होते हैं अर्थात् अपने स्वभावके परवश हुए कर्म करते हैं । ज्ञानवान् भी अपनी प्रकृतिके अनुसार चेष्टा करता है । फिर इसमें किसीका हठ क्या करेगा ? ॥
>
> Chapter 3 - verse 33

Your nature which is primarily anger, ego, and desire have been built over the years across many births. Your environment (good or bad) has been earned by your previous karmas. You see behaviour of some of the most successful people in their own fields. They are governed by their own nature. Some behave very arrogantly and despite the success they have, they seem to have no control on their nature. Some are very humble and polite and still very successful and even in the most challenging times; they never compromise with their behaviour.

These behaviours are built over births and have to be consciously controlled or changed during the lifetimes. It is not easy. That is why Krishna said that even the most intelligent people are slaves to their nature. Krishna consciousness will make you master of your nature in course of journey, not overnight.

For your upliftment, Krishna takes birth from time to time. He guides you on the right way. Bhagavad Gita is one great example of God's teachings to us for upliftment, to break the forecasts of behaviour of our nature and an opportunity to surprise God with your good deeds and thirst for upliftment. God is always looking for more and more people to come to his home or your home and always extends a helping hand for those wanting to go to Him. One fine day in your life, you decide to worship God and want him to listen to your prayers – be it a day or night – be it after 30 or 50 years of your life. But you expect that the day you decide to worship Him, He will listen to your prayers.

You never expect that God could say that I am also not available to accept worship for the next few years. If that happens, worlds will get ruined and destroyed. Look at His greatness that He just waits for you to come to Him all the time and He is always there to receive you. Start working on your nature – anger, ego and desire. Control on these can do wonders during this birth and after death. Bad nature if not controlled can put you on to a track where you may never be able to come back to the human birth for millions of years.

On the other hand control on your nature can put you on the right path towards God and you may get liberated within this birth or next birth will be happier and more peaceful than this birth to advance the journey further. Decision is yours.

God takes birth from time to time with a purpose

God needs to clean up the environment for the pious people from time to time and be an example for people on earth on how to live. Also, love from the individuals brings him down – such is the power of love and devotion. Way to God's home is in a different direction than way to the material world.

God does not write your karmas. But He knows your nature, so he knows how the world will behave. Many people take birth to advance their journey towards God. Birth of these people in any difficult environment is also due to their old karmas in previous births. When the general environment deteriorates, then it impacts the journey and meditation process of the humble people. God is always willing to extend all help to the people who want to go to Him irrespective of their previous karmas because He sees that people have fallen on the right track. So to help these people, He takes birth. The purpose of His birth is manifold.

His presence on earth in itself is a great blessing for the earth and brings in a great purification. He is also a role model for the people so that they can learn how to live and how to die. He eradicates the wrong doers from the earth and establishes religion on a firm footing that helps people advance their journey towards him. This way he also follows his defined rules for the earth. Mahabharata has been a great example. He killed many demons in his childhood to eradicate sinful people from the earth. But during the war of Mahabharata, Krishna did not engage in fight as he wanted to prove that right will win over the wrong eventually – he was the spiritual support to the right. With spiritual support which is always available to the right and only to the right – Right will always win. When Krishna took birth, just a handful of people knew that he was Lord. Till his departure from this earth, only a handful of people knew he was Lord and an incarnation of Vishnu. But today everyone knows that he was incarnation of God. Had he engaged in war, then this war would have been won by Lord. No, the message was that this war is to be won by the right over the wrong even when the wrong side was seen more powerful than right in the battlefield as army with wrong side was very strong. Many of them were highly blessed but this battle was the greatest proof that even the most blessed supporting a wrong cause get destroyed by God's system.

God's identity during their lifetime and appearance on earth remains a secret, it gets known to the common people only after their departure. Even devtas do not know the incarnation of God as God is above all. He gets known to those people whom He wishes that they should know Him. These people not only feel His presence when He takes birth but also see His presence within themself every moment.

> Lord says: Arjuna, whenever righteousness is on the decline, unrighteousness is in the ascendant, then I body Myself forth. For the protection of the virtuous, for the extirpation of evil-doers, and for establishing Dharma (righteousness) on a firm footing, I manifest Myself from age to age.
>
> हे भारत! जब-जब धर्मकी हानि और अधर्मकी वृद्धि होती है, तब-तब ही मैं अपने रूपको रचता हूँ अर्थात् साकाररूपसे लोगोंके सम्मुख प्रकट होता हूँ॥
>
> साधु पुरुषोंका उद्धार करनेके लिये, पापकर्म करनेवालोंका विनाश करनेके लिये और धर्मकी अच्छी तरहसे स्थापना करनेके लिये मैं युग-युगमें प्रकट हुआ करता हूँ॥
>
> Chapter 4 – verse 7 & 8

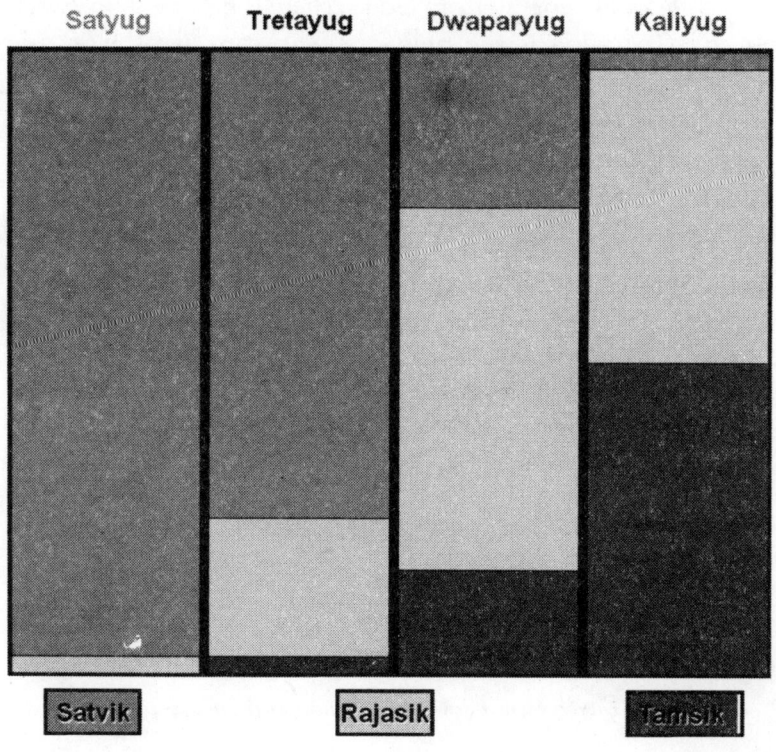

All souls draw life energy from God - There is no one in-between you and God. God is the only one who can give shelter and liberation. Guru can guide you to God's path but your own karmas will decide your destination.

Pitralok, Heaven, Human beings, Animals, Plants (Everyone) draws energy directly from Lord. Imagine the one who moves earth around sun at a speed more than 100,000 km. per hour.

Section 3

Death migration process

Krishna – Arjun

Soul carries intellect, mind, senses to the new body after death

Death – The ultimate truth – Migration process of soul to the new body. Soul carries the intellect, mind, karmas, and anger – ego – desire along to the new body.

Soul in the human body belongs to the Oversoul (God). Our soul draws energy from the Oversoul. It provides the life energy to the body. All souls are directly drawing energy from the Oversoul. There is no intermediary. All souls directly talk to God. All souls belong to God. So, if you take your identity as soul, then it never dies. That is what is conveyed in Bhagavad Gita that 'soul never dies'. It will never die even when all the worlds collapse one day because its home is beyond time which is never destroyed and that is God's home.

Physical Body is made of five elements - earth, air, fire, water and space and finally stays back on earth; and is cremated after the death.

Intelligence and Mind ride on the soul and migrate to the next birth that the soul takes.

Anger – Ego – Desire ride on the soul and migrate to the next birth that soul takes.

Feelings and Likings migrate with the soul to the next birth.

Attraction towards God – Rides very closely on the soul.

Karmas ride on the soul and go to the next birth that soul takes.

Soul is same in all human beings, animals, birds and other creatures. It is the combination of karmas, anger – ego – desire that decide the destination of the soul to the next body which could be higher worlds, i.e. devtas or it could be back on earth as human being or it could go to lower worlds of animals, etc.

> Lord says : Even as the wind wafts scents from their seat, so, too, the *Jivatma*, which is the controller of the body, etc. taking the mind and the senses from the body which it leaves behind, forthwith migrates to the body which it acquires.
>
> वायु गन्धके स्थानसे गन्धको जैसे ग्रहण करके ले जाता है, वैसे ही देहादिका स्वामी जीवात्मा भी जिस शरीरका त्याग करता है, उससे इन मनसहित इन्द्रियोंको ग्रहण करके फिर जिस शरीरको प्राप्त होता है—उसमें जाता है ॥
>
> Chapter 15- verse 8

Soul does not get contaminated, nor does it undergo any changes. It always remains pure; it could be seen as a carrier or God's representation and presence in every being.

Death migration process

Transfer on death

Physical body (Cremated) →

Material richness →

Rules of material world end here →   *Rules of spiritual world apply here* →

Spiritual Journey and attraction to God → ⇩ *Migrate to next birth*
Pious people start their next birth from where they left in last birth on spiritual journey

Karmas → ⇩ *Migrate to next birth*
Good karmas takes you to higher world, bad karmas to animal world

Intelligence and mind → ⇩ *Migrate to next birth*
Intelligence and Mind well interlocked result in good karmas and good next birth

Anger - Ego - Desire → ⇩ *Migrate to next birth*
Their degree of strength will decide birth in good or bad families and worlds

Likings and dislikings of senses → ⇩ *Migrate to next birth*
Sattvika takes you to higher worlds, rajasika to human worlds, tamasika to animals

Soul migrates to next birth and carries all of above   *Migrate to next birth*
Soul always stays pure and untouched by all.

Soul based on all above decides the next birth on to:
- God's home
- Higher worlds
- Human birth
- Animal world

Three destinations after death – higher worlds, human birth or lower worlds

Next birth will depend on your karmas during this birth and hence you yourself decide your next destination during this life in same way as you have decided your current birth.

There are three possible destinations after death

Higher Worlds - You could be liberated and reach Parbrahm which is God's home that we see as *Krishnalok*, Parbrahm, *Radhalok*, Golok, i.e. a place where time does not exist, a place that is self illumined, a place where sunshine does not reach. Some rare soul will go there and merge with God.

If you miss this destination, you may reach higher worlds that are seen as *Devlok* which is below time and ultimately will get destroyed by time some day unless devtas reach God's abode before that day. These devtas run the worlds for God and are in meditation and service to Lord.

These devtas also take birth as human beings but since they are very high souls, they choose birth in the religious and pious families. Their karmas help them select these families. The reason they take birth is because liberation happens much quicker from human birth. This is the gateway and a deciding birth that can take you in any destination – God's home, devtas, human birth or lower worlds.

Human Birth - Human birth is a blessing as this is the only birth where new karmas are allowed. It is rare. If you think, it will come easy again, it will not. You can yourself do a self evaluation as to where you will go. There are defined ways to measure your karmas and see where you are headed after the death.

Within human births, you have a lot of difference. You have people bestowed with intelligence, riches. You have people who are God realised souls. You have people suffering every day and unable to get their food and shelter. You have people who are regularly involved in criminal activities.

All these births are earnings from the karmas performed in the previous births and new karmas will decide the future births.

On a scale, human births will be one to million scale or rather the scale will be as big as the number of human beings since no two human beings are equal but still for analysis sake, you can categorise them in a defined number.

Lower Worlds - Lower worlds are worlds of hell, animals, birds and other lower world creatures. Fish live only in water. Snakes live on earth and water. Birds live on earth and can fly. These births are for suffering only. No new karmas are allowed in these births.

So, when an animal kills another animal as per his nature, he is not tainted in God's eyes. He also has the same soul as a human being and he may have been a human being in his earlier birth but got there because of his karmas performed during his human birth.

But in lower worlds, there is no good or bad karma – it is just suffering for a defined period. You could see this in God's constitution as a jail in these births for a defined period depending on the intensity of bad karmas.

The whole game revolves around karmas. Good karmas take you up, once you are up, there is a bigger opportunity to go further up. Bad karmas take you down , once you are down , quite likely that you may go further down because of the environment you get as a result of bad karmas is not as friendly as in your previous birth whereas the nature has further deteriorated.

When the nature deteriorates and the environment becomes more difficult, then there is a higher probability that a person will do more errors and sink down further.

So, now the game is about your determination that you want to do good karmas irrespective of the difficult and tough environment. This environment (friendly or not) is all your own earnings from the previous karmas, so no one else is to be blamed or appreciated for this situation but yourself.

Human birth sits on a hot seat. This birth is earned with a lot of difficulty. You should always be thankful to God for everything that he has given you. You could not ask or think of anything better. This feeling of thankfulness which will start with God will slowly start embedding in you. Then you will start thanking everyone for even smaller acts of help. This will make you humble. When you are humble and thankful, the nature starts supporting you and God starts supporting you as well. This support starts lifting you up and this is the journey towards God.

> Lord says: Those who abide in the quality of *Sattva* wend their way upwards; while those of a *Rajasika* disposition stay in the middle. And those of a *Tamasika* temperament, enveloped as they are in the effects of *Tamoguna*, sink down.
>
> सत्त्वगुणमें स्थित पुरुष स्वर्गादि उच्च लोकोंको जाते हैं, रजोगुणमें स्थित राजस पुरुष मध्यमें अर्थात् मनुष्यलोकमें ही रहते हैं और तमोगुणके कार्यरूप निद्रा, प्रमाद और आलस्यादिमें स्थित तामस पुरुष अधोगतिको अर्थात् कीट, पशु आदि नीच योनियोंको तथा नरकोंको प्राप्त होते हैं ॥
>
> Chapter 14 – verse 18

Death Migration Process

- No Anger, Ego, Desire, Mind and intellect interlocked.
- Always in Meditation.
- Satvik and Right Karmas.

God's Home - Above Time

Soul Missed God's Home

Below Time

Higher World of Devtas, Sun, Heaven, Pitralok

Heaven   Devtas & Pitralok   Sun

Falls down to human birth

- Anger, Ego, Desire.
- Mind and intellect not fully interlocked.
- Some Meditation, Rajasika and mixed Karmas.

Human Birth with attraction to God by Birth in a Pious Family - Nearest to God

Birth in Rich Families

Birth in Families where one works very hard and meets his basic needs.

Birth in Families where one works very hard and still cannot meet the basic needs.

Too much Anger, Ego, Desire, Tamasika Karmas Life spent in hurting others, inappropriate food habits, Bad Karmas

Lower worlds of Animals - Hellish World

Devoted soul that fails to reach God in current life gets more promising environment in next life for liberation

All human beings have equal opportunity to reach God within this birth though hardships and environment will vary from person to person which is due to the karmas of the previous births. Any committed and devoted person can reach him within this birth.

Human birth is very rare. This is the only birth where new karmas are allowed. This is the only birth that gives you the widest range of opportunities – one could go and merge with the Oversoul or one could go down to lower worlds of animals. Theory of karma looks simple but is too complex to understand and to follow. It is too deep but people with commitment and determination have passed through these phases in the past.

What is right and what is wrong – even people with highest intelligence may find themselves lost. So the first rule to follow is that you do not define your own rules. Follow the rules defined in the scriptures of your religion. Here also comes the importance for a guide. Bhagavad Gita is one of the guides for lifetime.

Now we are trying to explain below the various types of human births:

First Category – There are many human beings who work very hard day and night and are still not able to meet their basic needs of food and shelter, children education, and medical facilities. They have to struggle through life. These hardships are a result of previous karmas. When one is unable to meet his basic needs, one is prone to do an error or cheating. Once a person does the cheating, it means that he is doing bad karmas, as a result he falls down further in God's evaluation system.

This hard environment was not given to him by God but was the result of his own karmas. But once you do an error, it is adding to the list of your bad karmas which will take you down further. When the environment is not friendly then one has to be highly determined. People in this category may also be short of right education and good guides (Guru).

Second Category – There are human beings who work hard and can meet their basic needs. They also have to struggle though but they are better placed. Here again these people are prone to error for different reasons – for reasons of achievement more than their basic needs. So the intention or reason for error may change but may still exist. Result of error is same as bad karmas in God's system.

Third Category – There are people who are born in rich families and will never be short of their needs but they may or may not have an environment that will help them in progressing further on the journey towards God. They may have too many family demands or an environment of competition, jealousy, etc. They may be in a race for higher power, more money, etc. They are also prone to do an error for a totally different reason.

But the birth in this category is rare and a result of lot of good karmas. There is no need for people to do any error. They are intelligent, well educated, understand what is right and what is wrong and have earned a reasonably good environment. This category of people is most lost today under great influence of material world attraction.

Fourth Category – There are families that may not be very rich but are able to meet their basic needs well but the families have a very humble environment because they are learned and enlightened souls. These are highly respected families on earth and in God's eyes. This birth is very rare on earth as the souls here are the advanced souls for liberation and they also have the environment to help them progress on that path and they have the intelligence and mind well interlocked to work for liberation.

They know what liberation is and what binding is. Such birth comes only to a handful of rarest of rare souls who tried hard but missed reaching God in their earlier birth. These souls do not go to heaven which is a place for spending your good karmas and a waste of time in the eyes of a God realised soul. These souls defeat their journey through heaven and instead are born back on earth in these pious families to complete what they have missed in their previous birth.

> Lord says: Such a person who has strayed from Yoga, obtains the higher worlds, (heaven, etc.) to which men of meritorious deeds alone are entitled, and having resided there for innumerable years, takes birth of pious and prosperous parents.
>
> योगभ्रष्ट पुरुष पुण्यवानोंके लोकोंको अर्थात् स्वर्गादि उत्तम लोकोंको प्राप्त होकर, उनमें बहुत वर्षोंतक निवास करके फिर शुद्ध आचरणवाले श्रीमान् पुरुषोंके घरमें जन्म लेता है ॥
>
> Chapter 6 – verse 41

> Lord further says: Or, if he is possessed of dispassion, then not attaining to those regions he is born in the family of enlightened Yogis, but such a birth in this world is very difficult to obtain.
>
> अथवा वैराग्यवान् पुरुष उन लोकोंमें न जाकर ज्ञानवान् योगियोंके ही कुलमें जन्म लेता है। परन्तु इस प्रकारका जो यह जन्म है, सो संसारमें नि:सन्देह अत्यन्त दुर्लभ है ॥
>
> Chapter 6 – verse 42

This is rarest of the rare birth when you have the right environment, karmas, attraction towards God carried forward from your last birth – all supporting you for liberation. This birth is one of the last births before merger with God.

All the souls have opportunity for liberation. They can get liberation in any of the above categories. However the struggle is very different in each of the above births.

Also the attraction towards God is natural in the last category of births.

Higher you are in these categories, there is no need for you to do an error and there is a good opportunity that you can progress further upwards. A determined soul in the highest category may do no error and reach to the God, i.e. get liberated and a soul which is highly placed can also sink downwards if it is not careful about the karmas.

God's home and various types of births

God's home - Self Illumined - Above Time - All Peace

Time will destroy everything (below)

Time does not exist above this line   (Closest to God's home)

Sun, Devlok, Pitrlok, Heaven

Families of God realized souls
Rarest of rare births.
Human birth in pious families.
People just missed reaching God.
Brahman by karmas.

Heaven   Devtas & Pitralok   Sun

(Human birth on earth)

Rich families - Human births power families Kings
you see hundreds of rich and gifted people who are lost today as they are succumbed to Maya though they have excellent opportunity to advance journey towards God in this birth.

Human births - Difficult life but able to meet the basic needs

Human births - Difficult life unable to make both ends meet

All above this line have equal opportunity to reach God within this birth.

Lower worlds

Worlds of animals, Insects. Hell for people with bad karams
No new karmas are allowed, just sufferings for a defined period of life.

If you die as an angry person, you will be born as an angry person

You need to overcome your anger, ego and desire consciously within human birth. If they go very strong, they will encourage you to do an error and bad karmas. Bad karmas can lead your next birth in lower worlds of animals irrespective of the status you enjoy in your current birth.

> Lord says: From anger arises, delusion; from delusion confusion of memory; from confusion of memory, loss of reason; and from loss of reason one goes to complete ruin.
>
> क्रोधसे अत्यन्त मूढ़भाव उत्पन्न हो जाता है, मूढ़भावसे स्मृतिमें भ्रम हो जाता है, स्मृतिमें भ्रम हो जानेसे बुद्धि अर्थात् ज्ञानशक्तिका नाश हो जाता है और बुद्धिका नाश हो जानेसे यह पुरुष अपनी स्थितिसे गिर जाता है॥
>
> Chapter 2 - verse 63

In the soul migration process, intelligence and mind travel with soul to the next birth.

Anger, ego and desire are embedded on intelligence and mind. Soul stays pure and does not get impacted with anything. It is a carrier. It belongs to God (The ultimate truth).

Soul migrates to another body after death. If a person has been a very angry person through the life and was same at the time of death, soul will identify the right next birth for him based on his karmas.

An angry person may also have done lower karmas and will get into a body and family according to his karmas after the death. Depending on the intensity of anger and resultant bad karmas, next birth could well be a lower world's birth and may not be a human birth.

One has to leave the unwanted nature of high anger, ego and desire within his consciousness. This is not easy and needs a lot of determination and practice. Even after repeated practice and determination, one may not be successful because he did not have the right environment.

This environment is also the earning of karmas. So the task may be even more difficult. One needs to overcome this by accepting that what he got is based on his previous karmas and now is the opportunity to get rid of this unwanted nature and become a more humble person accepting the present environment.

Anger – Ego – Desire promote each other but the determined soul (one in thousand) can overcome his anger

Anger, Ego and Desire are three gates to hell. Minimise them if you wish to start the journey towards God. Anger, ego and desire can make one blind.

Reason why anger, ego and desire are called gates to hell is because they make you more prone to errors. They also promote each other. Error promotes error and slowly without knowledge one sinks deeper and deeper and finds it difficult to come out of it. These should be consciously worked upon and should be overcome with the help from strong and determined intelligence connected with mind.

Anger, ego and desire can make a person fall down to any level. You see uncountable number of people who are gifted with all the richness by God but have miserably fallen following these three gates to hell. People become angry even when they have no reason to go angry. One can increase his desires to any level that even this earth will fall short to meet one's expectations. Ego can make a person fall to any level. Intelligence knows all this but you still come under their control because you have not connected your intelligence with the mind.

A person with all the richness on this earth may be very poor because his desires are much more than what he has got. A poor man whose needs are limited to the very basic needs may think he is a very rich man. It is the difference between the visions of a God realised person who is always thankful to God versus a material hungry person who is always in search of more and can go down to any level to become materially richer. Bhagavad Gita gives a wake up call to these souls.

> Lord says: Desire, anger and greed – these triple gates of hell, bring about the downfall of the soul. Therefore, one should shun all these three.
>
> काम, क्रोध तथा लोभ—ये तीन प्रकारके नरकके द्वार आत्माका नाश करनेवाले अर्थात् उसको अधोगतिमें ले जानेवाले हैं। अतएव इन तीनोंको त्याग देना चाहिये॥
>
> Chapter 16 – verse 21

> Freed from these three gates of hell, man works for his own salvation and thereby attains the supreme goal, i.e. God.
>
> हे अर्जुन! इन तीनों नरकके द्वारोंसे मुक्त पुरुष अपने कल्याणका आचरण करता है, इससे वह परमगतिको जाता है अर्थात् मुझको प्राप्त हो जाता है॥
>
> Chapter 16 – verse 22

You may be one of the most intelligent and most logical persons on earth. You would have read many books that anger is one of the gates to hell. Try taking a decision that you will not get angry and you may miserably fail. There is a reason why one will fail. Many learned ones have tried this; it is not an easy thing to control. Anger does not come to you in one birth. You have accumulated anger over a period of many previous births. It may have fluctuated up and down in many births but it stayed with you. It is always looking for an opportunity to pop up. So, when you take a decision that you will not get angry, it does not matter to anger. It is there inside, it is deep rooted and it will find an opportunity to pop up.

The way to handle anger is different, not intellect alone. Intellect is the key driver for help, without intellect anger will not come under control but intellect needs the support of mind and determination. Still it is going to be a slow process which will depend on how deep rooted anger is and how determined are you to get rid of your anger.

Intelligence alone is not enough to help you overcome your anger, you need further shelter. This shelter may be different for different people in different environment. For some, they will take shelter under God and start meditation, this will help. Some may take shelter by helping the poor with their hard earnings, this will work. Some may just start giving more and more respect to elders and needy people, this will work too. Some may start creating a humble environment in their place of work and be helpful to the people they can, this will work.

The number of ways it will work is same as the number of human beings. Key is that sacrifice will work. Sacrifice is called *yagya*. You do not need to copy anyone; everyone has a direct path to God. As every soul is directly communicating to God with no one in between, it is exactly the same way that everyone can carve out his own path to reach God. But what you will notice is that once you carve out your own path, it may be very similar to paths that many others follow. Some on the meditation path, some on the silence path, some on helping others path, some on love and humble path and some on sharing path.

A learned soul sees God in everyone

Lord says: Those whose mind and Intellect are wholly merged in Him, who remain constantly established in identity with Him, and have finally become one with Him, their sins being wiped out by wisdom, reach the supreme goal whence there is no return.

जिनका मन तद्रूप हो रहा है, जिनकी बुद्धि तद्रूप हो रही है और सच्चिदानन्दघन परमात्मामें ही जिनकी निरन्तर एकीभावसे स्थिति है, ऐसे तत्परायण पुरुष ज्ञानके द्वारा पापरहित होकर अपुनरावृत्तिको अर्थात् परमगतिको प्राप्त होते हैं ॥

Chapter 5 - verse 17

The wise look with equanimity on all whether it be a *Brahmana* endowed with learning and humility, a cow, an elephant, a dog and a pariah, too.

वे ज्ञानीजन विद्या और विनययुक्त ब्राह्मणमें तथा गौ, हाथी, कुत्ते और चाण्डालमें भी समदर्शी ही होते हैं ॥

Chapter 5 - verse 18

When one goes through the purification, one starts seeing God in all his creations. This purification comes through humbleness, good karmas. It does not come to a person who has anger, ego or desire.

A God realised soul sees with the same eye a human being, a brahman, a cow or a *pariah*. The eyes in a God realised soul see the same God in every one. Such a soul is very rare. But you can find these human beings on earth, they are rare but they are among us just heading towards higher worlds after completing their natural duties in this birth. They are destined to reach God's home.

Everyone is engaged in duties. The one who sees all his duties as duties towards God becomes purified over the period of life.

This purification opens the eyes to the spiritual truth. A person engaged in material world will never be able to open his spiritual eyes.

One has to surrender to the God to get his blessings that will help in the journey towards God.

Source : www.bhagavad-gita.us

Section – 4

God's planning will overrule your planning

Maa Durga

God realised soul gets knowledge from within

God realised soul does not need any books or religious knowledge. Books are too elementary for that person as soul starts showing the light to that individual. Best knowledge is the knowledge that is learnt from inside. Scriptures teach you how to invoke the inner self – purity enables you.

> Lord says: A Brahmana, who has obtained enlightenment, has as much use for all the Vedas as one who stands at the brink of a sheet of water overflowing on all sides has for a small reservoir of water.
>
> सब ओरसे परिपूर्ण जलाशयके प्राप्त हो जानेपर छोटे जलाशयमें मनुष्यका जितना प्रयोजन रहता है, ब्रह्मको तत्त्वसे जाननेवाले ब्राह्मणका समस्त वेदोंमें उतना ही प्रयोजन रह जाता है॥
>
> Chapter 2 - verse 46

All Vedas have been created by God. He is the source of Vedas. We follow Vedas as guide for our lives. One can keep reading Vedas through life and follow the teachings. Vedas guide you for all the righteous things. If one can reach the source which is God, then one does not need to read the Vedas.

How to reach the source? Different people crafted different paths to reach the source. Source is sitting inside and can be reached with internal purity, meditation, right karmas and unequal love and devotion to God. One good starting point of this journey is jaap yagya (among yagya's Krishna has identified Himself as jaap yagya).

Once one reaches the source and is able to realise his presence within – one does not need to read any scriptures. Further knowledge starts pouring from within. This soul does not go wrong and does not need any guidance. It is important to find that source within through purity, love, sacrifice and meditation. One who realises his presence through purity is Brahman by karma and is entitled to merge with him by advancing the journey further.

If you see a child, an elderly person or a sufferer in pain and it invokes the same pain in you, it means that realisation of his presence is not far. He feels the pain of everyone and when it also comes in you, it means that identity has started getting established with Him and unity with Him is not very far. If the same thing brings no change in you, it means you need to cover some journey.

Self Evaluation – Where one is heading after death

We can ourselves evaluate where we are heading after death. If sattvika dominates, one is headed for Higher Worlds. If Rajasika dominates, one is headed back for the human birth and if Tamasika dominates, then one is headed for lower worlds of animals.

Everyone has one of the three feelings coming up at any time during the day and night. These three feelings are called

1. Sattvika - Mode of Goodness
2. Rajasika - Mode of Passion
3. Tamasika - Mode of Darkness or ignorance

When **sattvika** dominates, you will have a feeling of goodness. You will like the surroundings, you will like the nature, and you will like the people around you, no feeling of jealousy, ego, desire, and anger. Everything is good. Your mind will be at peace. You will have no complaints what soever. You want to help people. You like natural food.

When **Rajasika** dominates, you will be disturbed. You will have feelings like anger, ego, desire, and jealousy. You may have many complaints in your mind. You will have a lot of love for money, lot of worldly desires. Feelings of hatred will show up. You are restless, you need more. You have many tasks to complete that will bring in more material benefits. Rajasika people have more attraction towards spicy foods, fried foods, and deep cooked foods.

When **Tamasika** dominates, you will want to hurt someone, cause injury to people, cheat and insult others. Tamasika person loses the differentiation between what is right and what is wrong. In Tamasika attitude, the wrong thing also seems to be right. One starts following his own defined set of wrong rules.

What will dominate on you at the time of death will be same as that has been working on you for a greater part of your life and more importantly during the later life before death.

Kings and most of the people during older times used to leave for forests after the age of seventy five with a determination of not coming back to the kingdom but leave their lives (bodies) on earth in the forests. These were people of intellect who understood these three feelings. They were determined to prepare well for the next birth. Their aim was to get the domination of sattvika on them during the last leg of their life with help from meditation and sacrifice.

God owns all and needs all – Higher Worlds, human beings and Lower Worlds. God will always want to guide you towards the path to his home. It is one's nature and karma (in a way they are highly linked and interlocked) that will determine where you finally reach.

The soul inside everyone – higher worlds, human birth and lower worlds belongs to God who is beyond time. So home for everyone is same, i.e. God's Home. Sooner you can get back, better you will feel.

> Lord says: Only the Purusa in association with Prakrti experiences objects of the nature of the three *Gunas* evolved from Prakrti and it is attachment with these Gunas that is responsible for the birth of this soul in good and evil wombs.
>
> प्रकृतिमें स्थित ही पुरुष प्रकृतिसे उत्पन्न त्रिगुणात्मक पदार्थोंको भोगता है और इन गुणोंका संग ही इस जीवात्माके अच्छी-बुरी योनियोंमें जन्म लेनेका कारण है ॥
>
> प्रकृति शब्दका अर्थ भगवान्‌की त्रिगुणमयी माया से है।
>
> सत्त्वगुणके संगसे देवयोनिमें एवं रजोगुणके संगसे मनुष्य-योनिमें और तमोगुणके संगसे पशु, पक्षी आदि नीच योनियोंमें जन्म होता है।
>
> Chapter 13 - verse 21

Going by the results, one's life should be focused on sattvika karmas and renunciation. Sattvika is humble and takes one upwards but in absence of renunciation, sattvika can take one to heaven. Without renunciation, it will not be able to take you to God's home. So, one has to adapt all sattvika habits and renunciation as that will give you the path to God's home. Rajasika will bring you back as a human being and you will be one of the billions on the earth.

God's scale of human beings is one is to billion as every human being is different like everyone's face is different; everyone's karmas are different from others. Tamasika karmas will take one to the lower births and one will be there for uncountable number of years.

There is no relief once one ends up there as no new karmas are allowed. As a tiger, whether one kills animals or does not kill animals no way is monitored for a reward or an early relief from that life of lower worlds. Once there, it is defined for a number of years for which one needs to live in those lower worlds. Ignorance is tamasika.

> Lord says: Of these, Sattva being immaculate, is illuminating and flawless, Arjuna; it binds through attachment to happiness and knowledge.
>
> हे निष्पाप! उन तीनों गुणोंमें सत्त्वगुण तो निर्मल होनेके कारण प्रकाश करनेवाला और विकाररहित है, वह सुखके सम्बन्धसे और ज्ञानके सम्बन्धसे अर्थात् उसके अभिमानसे बाँधता है॥
>
> Chapter 14 – verse 6
>
> Arjuna, know the quality of Rajas, which is of the nature of passion, as born of desire and attachment. It binds the soul through attachment to actions and their fruit.
>
> हे अर्जुन! रागरूप रजोगुणको कामना और आसक्तिसे उत्पन्न जान। वह इस जीवात्माको कर्मोंके और उनके फलके सम्बन्धसे बाँधता है॥
>
> Chapter 14 – verse 7

> And know Tamas, the deluder of all those who look upon the body as their own self, as born of ignorance. It binds the soul through error, sleep and sloth, Arjuna.
>
> हे अर्जुन! सब देहाभिमानियोंको मोहित करनेवाले तमोगुणको तो अज्ञानसे उत्पन्न जान। वह इस जीवात्माको प्रमाद, आलस्य और निद्राके द्वारा बाँधता है॥
>
> Chapter 14 - verse 8
>
> Lord says: Sattva draws one to joy and Rajas to action; while Tamas, clouding wisdom, impels one to error, sleep and sloth Arjuna.
>
> हे अर्जुन! सत्त्वगुण सुखमें लगाता है और रजोगुण कर्ममें तथा तमोगुण तो ज्ञानको ढककर प्रमादमें भी लगाता है॥
>
> Chapter 14 - verse 9

Most of the human beings are struck in rajasika and tamasika acts. When one is unable to differentiate between rajasika and tamasika, more likely that one out of ignorance is deeper into tamasika. Rajasika is desire to earn more, spend more, leisure more – all enjoyments. When all this is done at the cost of hurting someone, unlawfully and unintelligently, the same thing becomes tamasika.

Few intelligent people who have been successful in connecting the intelligence with the mind will go to the sattvika path.

Same job, same work, same duties, earnings can be done in all the three ways – Sattvika, Rajasika and Tamasika. In sattvika mode – one will create a pleasant feeling and environment all around, it will be full of trust and all results will be left to God and when you leave the results to God, the results will be much better than the ones you can produce (which is also produced with God's blessing though you are ignorant about it).

In Rajasika mode – in the same environment – you create restlessness, over work, focus on producing more results – compromise on the truthfulness. Once you create that environment, that environment is carried by the people farther and this spreads more and more and you are the responsible source for that environment.

In Tamasika again, you do the same things with anger, hurt, and error through ignorance. You create an environment of cheating, unlawful activities. You spread hatred. Results will be very unpleasant both during this life and after death.

Sattvika will go a long way. Rajasika will be short lived and tamasika will be just ignorance. All three feelings and modes, i.e. sattvika, rajasika and tamasika are present in every individual all the time and they struggle with each other. sattvika drives one to humbleness, truthfulness, and goodness. Even in sattvika person, rajasika and tamasika feelings will dominate but that will be for very short period and may not leave any impact on his personality. This person is sattvika dominated and is getting ready for higher worlds or God's Home.

Rajasika drives one to hoarding more and more pleasures and work accordingly but without error. In rajasika person – sattvika feelings will also dominate for some duration and tamasika will also try to dominate. Tamasika drives one to error, sleep. Tamasika also tries to dominate sattvika and rajasika.

There is a struggle between all three for supremacy.

> Lord says: Overpowering Rajas and Tamas, Sattva prevails; overpowering Sattva and Tamas, Rajas prevails: even so, overpowering Sattva and Rajas, Tamas prevails.
>
> हे अर्जुन! रजोगुण और तमोगुणको दबाकर सत्त्वगुण, सत्त्वगुण और तमोगुणको दबाकर रजोगुण, वैसे ही सत्त्वगुण और रजोगुणको दबाकर तमोगुण होता है अर्थात् बढ़ता है ॥
>
> Chapter 14 – verse 10

This has a very important message that all the three forces are always trying to dominate, you need to work on making sattvika dominate most of the time. All will dominate during some part of the day, what matters is which dominates on you most of the time. Also tamasika should not dominate with its aggression, as that can lead to some unrepairable results.

God's home

Above Time

Sattvika + Renunciation takes one to God's home (Sattvika + Meditation + Renunciation)

Meditation

Sattvika pull - pure heart, pure mind, heart and mind are connected, eats pure food, God loving, meditates

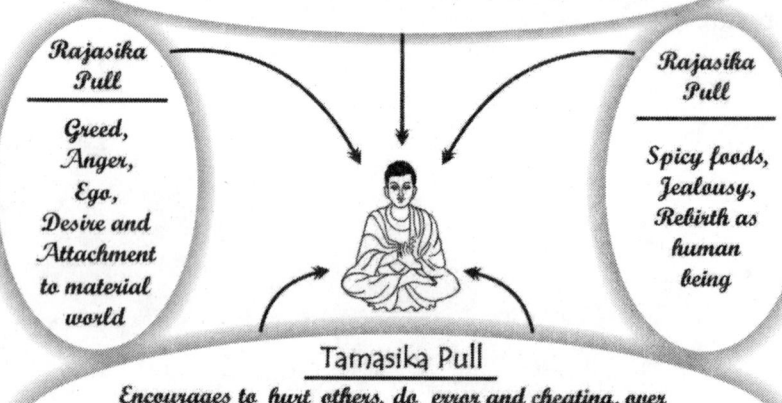

Rajasika Pull

Greed, Anger, Ego, Desire and Attachment to material world

Rajasika Pull

Spicy foods, Jealousy, Rebirth as human being

Tamasika Pull

Encourages to hurt others, do error and cheating, over sleep, intoxication, consume impure food, selfishness, steals livehood of others (Will take one to animal world after death)

Human being is pulled by Sattvika, Rajasika and Tamasika all the time

Lord says: When light and discernment dawn in this body, as well as in the mind and senses, then one should know that Sattva is predominant.

जिस समय इस देहमें तथा अन्तःकरण और इन्द्रियोंमें चेतनता और विवेकशक्ति उत्पन्न होती है, उस समय ऐसा जानना चाहिये कि सत्त्वगुण बढ़ा है ॥

Chapter 14 – verse 11

With the preponderance of Rajas, Arjuna, greed, activity, undertaking of action with an interested motive, restlessness and a thirst for enjoyment make their appearance.

हे अर्जुन! रजोगुणके बढ़नेपर लोभ, प्रवृत्ति, स्वार्थबुद्धिसे कर्मोंका सकामभावसे आरम्भ, अशान्ति और विषयभोगोंकी लालसा—ये सब उत्पन्न होते हैं ॥

Chapter 14 – verse 12

With the growth of Tamas, Arjuna, obtuseness of the mind and senses, disinclination to perform one's obligatory duties, frivolity and stupor – all these appear.

हे अर्जुन! तमोगुणके बढ़नेपर अन्तःकरण और इन्द्रियोंमें अप्रकाश, कर्तव्य-कर्मोंमें अप्रवृत्ति और प्रमाद अर्थात् व्यर्थ चेष्टा और निद्रादि अन्तःकरणकी मोहिनी वृत्तियाँ—ये सब ही उत्पन्न होते हैं ॥

Chapter 14 – verse 13

One can very well monitor domination of goodness, passion and ignorance throughtout the day. If you are a peaceful and loving person, you normally will be at peace even in unfavourable circumstances. It does not mean that you will not get agitated at times. Sattvika is dominating on you most of the time but Rajasika (desires) and tamasika (feeling of hurting and ignorance) also dominate for short durations.

On the other hand, if desires are always riding high on you making you angry and restless, then rajasika is dominating on you most of the time. The same person will also have feelings of goodness about people, environment at times – it means sattvika is dominating for that duration. He will also be taking unpleasant decisions of hurting the livelihood of some people which means tamasika is dominating for that duration. All three will try to create their supremacy on you. If you let sattvika ride on you for greater duration – you are headed for higher worlds. Rajasika domination will bring you back to the human birth and tamasika domination will take you to the lower worlds.

All this is also clubbed with one's karmas. If one's karmas are too bad, then one is headed towards lower worlds. Within Rajasika, even when you come back to earth as a human being, karmas will decide what type of birth you take – whether in a humble and pious family or rich and aristocratic family or in a poor environment.

One who conquers his mind and is on sattvika path is a deserving individual to advance the journey towards God's home.

Domination of modes at the time of death decides the next birth

Domination of modes of goodness, passion and ignorance at the time of death take an individual to higher worlds, human beings and lower worlds of animals in the next birth.

Destination after death is dependent on what dominates on an individual at the time of death – sattvika, rajasika or tamasika.

What will dominate will be one that has been dominating for most of his life time.

Lord says: When a man dies during the preponderance of Sattva, he obtains the stainless ethereal worlds (heaven, etc.,) attained by men of noble deeds.

जब यह मनुष्य सत्त्वगुणकी वृद्धिमें मृत्युको प्राप्त होता है, तब तो उत्तम कर्म करनेवालोंके निर्मल दिव्य स्वर्गादि लोकोंको प्राप्त होता है ॥

Chapter 14 – verse 14

Dying when Rajas predominates, he is born among those attached to action; even so, the man who has expired during the preponderance of Tamas is reborn in the species of the deluded creatures such as insects and beasts, etc.

रजोगुणके बढ़नेपर मृत्युको प्राप्त होकर कर्मोंकी आसक्तिवाले मनुष्योंमें उत्पन्न होता है; तथा तमोगुणके बढ़नेपर मरा हुआ मनुष्य कीट, पशु आदि मूढ़योनियोंमें उत्पन्न होता है ॥

Chapter 14 – verse 15

If one wants to reach God's home, then one has to adopt all sattvika habits. There cannot be a compromise, i.e. that one decides to have good feelings and work towards good for everyone but decides not to change his food habits. Food habits alone will bring one down. Sattvika is a friend of sattvika – so feelings, actions, food, thoughts, karmas all have to go hand in hand.

Also sattvika food habits will support sattvika actions otherwise there will be a conflict and it will bring the person down from sattvika to rajasika/tamasika. If one is not a complete sattvika – then one does not get unconditional support from the sattvika system, so one may fall short in completing the journey to God within one birth though that person may still have a more promising next birth to complete the journey from where it was left due to all other sattvika habits.

Remember, if you are on a journey towards God and you could not reach the destination in your current life then in the next birth one starts from the same point and one may further advance and reach God in the next birth or it can happen reverse also, that one may start a reverse journey in the next birth by getting attracted more to the material world. This is Maya which can drive you in a reverse direction so you need his blessings to overcome his Maya (Maya is also his creation). Jaap (chanting his holy name) will clear the inner darkness and help one reach his home while duly performing his natural duties. As Krishna says that among all yagyas (acts of sacrifice), I am the jaap yagya. Lord has placed jaap yagya above all the yagyas.

Krishna told Arjun that having understood the truth, one should not leave any moment where one is not advancing his journey towards God because you never know about the next birth's environment, i.e. environment will be very promising without doubt but one can get attracted towards material things. That is why devtas are also afraid of taking birth in human life as Maya forces are very strong and they know about these forces but they have no other choice as way to God goes fastest from human life due to larger opportunities for sacrifice.

Such is the beautiful asset you got without realising the real value of this asset. So, Krishna advised – try your best to cover the journey within one birth because now you have the realisation of God's home. Do not waste your time in material attraction; you do not know what you are losing.

Sattvika, rajasika and tamasika dominate at the time of death. Sattvika, rajasika and tamasika are also directly related to good, mixed and bad karmas.

Sattvika dominates

- Pure and natural food likings
- No feeling of jealousy.
- Attracted towards God
- No Anger, Ego, Desire Helping others.

Destination - Higher worlds

Rajasika dominates

- Likes spicy pungent food
- Material attraction
- Restlessness
- Degree of Anger, Ego, Desire is more.
- Prone to errors

Destination - Human birth

Human birth with attraction to God by birth in a pious family - Nearest to God.

Birth in rich families

Birth in families where one works very hard and meets his basic needs.

Birth in families where one works very hard and still can't meet the basic needs.

Tamasika dominates

- Liking for overripe, stale and unnatural food.
- Hurts others
- likes sleeping, lethargic, snatches others livelihood.
- Full of Anger, Ego, Desire.
- Does not believe in God

Destination - Animals and hellish worlds

Surrender to God for renunciation

One has to rise above all the three *gunas* to reach God – All three gunas (sattvika, rajasika and tamasika) are binding in good or bad way. One has to adopt sattvika habits and then go for renunciation. Renunciation cannot go with rajasika or tamasika gunas. Also just one of the rajasika or tamasika habits is enough to pull a person down.

Now comes the importance of going above all the three modes of nature as all three modes have a binding. That comes through renunciation to the sattvika people. That does not come to rajasika and tamasika. So you need to go for renunciation following sattvika habits.

Renunciation will come only when you take shelter under Him through meditation, chanting His holy name and prayer – It will not come by taking a decision alone. Maya is more powerful than your decision because it is Maya which is his creation so do not get over confident on your intelligence – Seek His blessings through meditation and *bhakti*. Sattvika is goodness. It takes you to heaven so that you can reap the fruits of your good deeds. When the merits are exhausted, you fall back on earth in a rich family with everything gifted by birth. You still go through the natural pains realised through birth, death, old age, and disease. Rajasika is inferior to sattvika and brings you back to human birth faster than sattvika and does not give you as friendly and rich environment as sattvika. Tamasika takes one to the lower worlds.

Renunciation means working with no attachment to results of your actions. That means you get rid of desires. When you get rid of desires, you actually also get rid of anger and ego. Renunciation will come with His blessings, when you have faith in him and you leave everything on to him. And trust him and trust his system, it will never go wrong, it has never gone wrong. Just have faith in him. Love him with undivided attention and he will take care of your needs for the spiritual journey.

> Lord says: The whole of this creation is deluded by these objects evolved from the three modes of Prakrti – Sattva, Rajas and Tamas; that is why the world fails to recognise Me, standing apart from these, the Imperishable.
>
> गुणोंके कार्यरूप सात्त्विक, राजस और तामस— इन तीनों प्रकारके भावोंसे यह सारा संसार— प्राणिसमुदाय मोहित हो रहा है, इसीलिये इन तीनों गुणोंसे परे मुझ अविनाशीको नहीं जानता ॥
>
> Chapter 7 – verse13
>
> For, this most wonderful Maya (veil) of Mine, consisting of the three Gunas (modes of Nature) is extremely difficult to breakthrough; this, however, who constantly adore Me alone, are able to cross it.
>
> क्योंकि यह अलौकिक अर्थात् अति अद्भुत त्रिगुणमयी मेरी माया बड़ी दुस्तर है; परन्तु जो पुरुष केवल मुझको ही निरन्तर भजते हैं, वे इस मायाको उल्लंघन कर जाते हैं अर्थात् संसारसे तर जाते हैं ॥
>
> Chapter 7 – verse 14

Here God has clearly stated that the ones who constantly worship me can surpass the bindings of sattvika, rajasika and tamasika.

Meditation can do wonders and can get you rid of past sins of many births in this very birth. Start practising it without wasting any time. Nothing can replace meditation. Nothing can give you pleasure that mediation and love for God can give. Nothing can liberate you other than meditation.

Meditation (chanting God's holy name) alone can put you to the right path.

> Lord says: He too who, constantly worships Me through the Yoga of exclusive devotion – transcending these three Gunas, he becomes eligible for attaining Brahma.
>
> और जो पुरुष अव्यभिचारी भक्तियोगके द्वारा मुझको निरन्तर भजता है, वह भी इन तीनों गुणोंको भलीभाँति लाँघकर सच्चिदानन्दघन ब्रह्मको प्राप्त होनेके लिये योग्य बन जाता है॥
>
> Chapter 14 – verse 26

Embrace your current environment whole heartedly

Not accepting the current environment will drive you to error which will take you further down from where you are today. By accepting it you can move up very fast.

If you find fault in your current environment at home or at your workplace and you take that as a reason for not being able to move up towards God, then you will never be able to move up. Because of the environment, you will not do meditation, you may do error, you may fight back at home or in office or in society for little reasons – all these will add to your list of bad karmas which will bring you down further in the next birth. You will have to accept the current environment 'As it is' and then find a way to move up. This way even if you do not reach God, you will get a more friendly environment in your next birth that will help you move up.

Attraction towards God/Meditation flows with you to the next birth. Meditation can help you stay calm in any environment and can also turn your environment to more friendly environment. Meditation can kill anger – ego – desire – jealousy, in fact, all the unwanted habits and meditation will also help move in the journey towards God. Your current environment is your own earning by karmas of your previous births.

You can reach God within this life

If you are sincere in your search for God and your love is true (not for material gains), then all the right karmas of your previous births come in support for your liberation to God's home.

> Lord says: The Yogi, however, who diligently takes up the practice, attains perfection in this very life with the help of latencies of many births, and being thoroughly purged of sin, forthwith reaches the supreme state.
>
> परन्तु प्रयत्नपूर्वक अभ्यास करनेवाला योगी तो
> पिछले अनेक जन्मोंके संस्कारबलसे इसी जन्ममें
> संसिद्ध होकर सम्पूर्ण पापोंसे रहित हो फिर तत्काल
> ही परमगतिको प्राप्त हो जाता है ॥
>
> Chapter 6 - verse 45

This verse has a beautiful meaning. If one works sincerely to attain God and overcomes all the worldly desires, he gets support from all the good karmas of his previous births. These good karmas of previous births get invoked and work in support of the deserving soul to reach God's home within this birth.

You have a stock of good karmas and bad karmas. Their influence on you changes your behaviour in this birth. If your behaviour goes very humble and pious and you are in meditation and devotional path, then stock of all good karmas of past many births will immediately come in support and lift you up as you need their support for liberation.

God is always working

Importance of karma – God who needs nothing is always working. If God stops working, so will we as soul draws energy and direction from Oversoul.

> Lord says: Arjuna, there is no duty in all the three worlds for Me to perform, nor is there anything worth attaining, unattained by Me; yet I continue to work.
>
> हे अर्जुन! मुझे इन तीनों लोकोंमें न तो कुछ कर्तव्य है और न कोई भी प्राप्त करनेयोग्य वस्तु अप्राप्त है, तो भी मैं कर्ममें ही बरतता हूँ॥
>
> Should I not engage in action scrupulously at any time, great harm will come to the world; for, Arjuna, men follow My way in all matters.
>
> क्योंकि हे पार्थ! यदि कदाचित् मैं सावधान होकर कर्मोंमें न बरतूँ तो बड़ी हानि हो जाय; क्योंकि मनुष्य सब प्रकारसे मेरे ही मार्गका अनुसरण करते हैं॥
>
> If I ever cease to act, these worlds would perish; nay, I should prove to be the cause of confusion, and of the destruction of these people.
>
> इसलिये यदि मैं कर्म न करूँ तो ये सब मनुष्य नष्ट-भ्रष्ट हो जायँ और मैं संकरताका करनेवाला होऊँ तथा इस समस्त प्रजाको नष्ट करनेवाला बनूँ॥
>
> Chapter 3 – verse 22, 23, 24

All souls are connected with Oversoul all the time. Soul is always in constant dialogue with Oversoul even while we are not aware of it. Soul is always recording what we are saying, what we are doing. Soul is a carrier of our karmas, intelligence and mind to next birth – be it a merger with God, be it a place in higher worlds, be it a birth again as a human being or be it a birth in the lower world of insects and animals.

Soul in consultation with Oversoul decides the migration. While we see death of a human being, Oversoul does not see it as a death. It sees the migration of soul from one birth and body to the next one.

When we sleep or when we are awake, our nervous system is always working. Our heart is working. This system draws living energy from the soul. Our body draws the physical energy from food, air, water, etc. But at the time of death, despite all things being available, the body stops functioning as soul has moved out of the body that kept the system going. One loses the *chetna* (Consciousness).

This soul is no different than God. If Oversoul stops working, then all the souls drawing energy from the God's system will get confused and will start losing their purpose. Since soul is always connected with the God, God's system needs to be always functional as a guide.

Hence Krishna says that I keep working all the time. If I do not work, then these souls connected with me will see that Oversoul is not working and they will also stop working even if they keep getting the energy to stay live.

So, Krishna has to be the model for all the souls for many purposes, i.e. to keep them live so that the system keeps going and to show them the right path always for liberation. Impact of Maya takes us away from God's path. Two paths move in opposite direction – Way to God's home and way to material world.

That is why, to know liberation and then to get the liberation, you must know soul as that is the only way to get connected with Oversoul. There are many ways for an individual to connect with the soul. These ways will depend on one's way of life, environment and an individual's collection of past karmas.

A Sanyasi will know soul through inner finding and purity – may be living away from world in a lonely place through meditation. A person in family life – be it father or a mother will recognise soul by doing all their natural duties rightfully through sacrifice and yet meditating on God all the time.

An intelligent person will find him through the right use of his intelligence for society which is God's world and making sure that through his intelligence, people working with him and talking to him have something to gain spiritually also. He creates a humble environment all around and takes on the meditation. A simple housewife may find him through prayers, meditation, and love while doing all her duties towards children, elderly people and others at home. Some may find him just through love. *Gopis* reached him through sheer selfless love. That is the most beautiful journey with even more beautiful destination.

You do not need to follow anyone as your nature and his nature may not be same, you need to understand yourself and follow the right path towards him. You will need guidance on the right path. Do not write your own rules and declare yourself as the winner, these may not be His rules of the game. Take advise from scriptures.

All scriptures will guide you towards the right path – religion does not matter. You may have a Guru who will set you on the right path, i.e. you can have Bhagavad Gita as your Guru as it has all answers for people with different nature, lifestyle and environment.

God's planning will overrule your planning

Right karma is supreme and the quickest way to reach God. Karma decides your life now and destiny after death. Your previous karmas had decided your current birth and environment.

> Lord says: Your right is to work only and never to the fruit thereof. Do not consider yourself to be the cause of the fruit of action; nor let your attachment be to inaction.
>
> तेरा कर्म करनेमें ही अधिकार है, उसके फलोंमें कभी नहीं । इसलिये तू कर्मोंके फलका हेतु मत हो तथा तेरी कर्म न करनेमें भी आसक्ति न हो ॥
>
> Chapter 2 – verse 47

This verse is heart of Bhagavad Gita teachings. It has the key message from Lord Krishna.

Your right is to perform your prescribed duties and you should not worry about the fruits of the actions. God's message is: God has a system to rightfully give you the fruits of your actions and you should not work on deciding the fruits of your actions. You do not need to worry in the area where God has taken His personal responsibility and ownership. Do not interfere in His system as that system is flawless, it will work, we need to focus on our work and our duties, as God is the knower of all our past births and our past karmas (Actions).

Your current birth was decided by God's system. God has decided this birth for you or you could also say that your karma decided this birth for you. God's system was facilitator doing the justice in his own defined system. Now this became your natural duty as you were born in your current environment.

> Lord says: From whom all beings come into being and by whom the whole universe is pervaded, by worshipping Him through the performance of his natural duties, man attains the highest perfection.
>
> जिस परमेश्वरसे सम्पूर्ण प्राणियोंकी उत्पत्ति हुई है और जिससे यह समस्त जगत् व्याप्त है, उस परमेश्वरकी अपने स्वाभाविक कर्मोंद्वारा पूजा करके मनुष्य परमसिद्धिको प्राप्त हो जाता है ॥
>
> Chapter 18 – verse 46

If you have taken birth in a business family, then your natural duty is that you do your business in a very pure and truthful manner. If you are holding a position where you decide the fate of many people, then your duty is to uplift the people working with you and at the same time serve the organisation rightfully that pays for your bread and for your people's bread. Create an environment that is liked by God while you stay focused on your right work. The environment you create will be spread further by the people you impact (i.e. by the people working with you), so you may become a source or inspiration of creating a particular environment within your range.

If you are sitting in a corporate world at a high position and you create an environment of tension and anger, it does not stay limited to you but people who work with you create the same environment with their teams as well as their families. Family members then get influenced by the same environment and spread it further in the society – unknowingly you may be doing such damage to the morale and upbringing of so many people, housewives and children. If you create a humble environment of mutual trust and respect, then that may spread across like the earlier one and you may be doing well to so many people in the society.

If you think, you can produce better results by anger and mistrust – think again – you are living in God's system and if you create such an environment, you will get no support from God's system. Your support will come from the material world whose principles are written by humans, so the results are short lived and may not be pleasant at the end.

If you are a house wife, then you must see that your children are getting the food in time, they are getting the right spiritual education (*Sanskur*) in addition to their regular education. Elders are getting the right food and attention. You have the duty to see that your house is run in a spiritual manner. You may be a rich person and have many servants, that does not reduce your duty; it only changes the type of duty within the home. You still need to supervise, feed children with your own hands, teach them good deeds personally. Remember that seeds you sow, you will end up reaping in later life and future births. Also remember that this whole system sits on sacrifice, without sacrifice, you will not reach anywhere.

If you try to run the complete home system with money by having servants to take care of all the needs of your children , then children's responsibilities (when they grow up) will also be limited to take care of you with money at the time you may need them more than money, i.e. (during your old age and period of difficulty). Do not develop a money system. It will hurt you at the end of your life and the disturbance will impact your nature, karmas and hence future births.

God looked at your karma's and then decided your current birth. Still, He is giving a rich man, a poor man or a handicapped man an equal opportunity for liberation. It is only that some have difficult environment and some have very friendly environment.

This environment is also your own earning based on your past karmas. Now if you are in a difficult environment and you perform your duties poorly, you will fall further down. So it requires a commitment to reach Him and that is when you will find things easy as you are receving His help all the time. So remember him all the time in every circumstance. Results are not in your hand. Results are in hands of your karmas but since He is the Supreme one, He can help you erase your bad karmas; you need to surrender your self to Him. The things in your hand are prayers, chanting His holy name, good karmas.

> Lord says: Wielding My Nature I procreate again and again , according to their respective Karmas , all this multitude of beings subject to the sway of their own nature.
>
> अपनी प्रकृतिको अंगीकार करके स्वभावके बलसे परतन्त्र हुए इस सम्पूर्ण भूतसमुदायको बार-बार उनके कर्मोंके अनुसार रचता हूँ॥
>
> Chapter 9 – verse 8

Lord Krishna clearly states that all the births in different worlds and families are a result of individuals good and bad karmas. He is the creator but we write our own destiny under His defined constitution. Scriptures guides us on that constitution, so we should not define our own rules.

Lord Krishna has put renunciation of fruits of all actions above meditation because renunciation will bring peace of mind. Such a soul by nature will get attracted towards God because as you remove the dirt and other heaviness of anger, ego and desire from the soul, it starts showing itself to you and by the flawless nature you will get attracted towards God.

So a person engaged in right karmas and renunciation is going to get God's meditation internally because soul is no different than God and all that you were looking from the scriptures, you suddenly find sitting inside you and pouring from inside. That is the highest state of meditation and journey towards God's home.

Internal purification is must to start the journey towards God

Internal purification is must for upliftment. Unless you purify your innerself, journey towards God will not even start despite all your efforts. With purification – all secrets and knowledge about God start pouring from within. That is the state when one needs no books and no scriptures. Bhagavad Gita is sitting inside everyone.

> Lord said : Striving Yogis too are able to realise this Self enshrined in their heart. The ignorant, however, whose heart has not been purified, know not this Self inspite of their best endeavors.
>
> यत्न करनेवाले योगीजन भी अपने हृदयमें स्थित इस आत्माको तत्त्वसे जानते हैं; किन्तु जिन्होंने अपने अन्तःकरणको शुद्ध नहीं किया है, ऐसे अज्ञानीजन तो यत्न करते रहनेपर भी इस आत्माको नहीं जानते ॥
>
> Chapter 15 - verse 11

Journey towards God's home will not start without internal purification. Purification process and how to start it depends a lot on your nature, your habits, your environment and your likings. You need to understand yourself and not copy others.

If you are an intelligent person and always busy – be it job or be it business or be it any other profession. You may not have time for meditation and you may not like to listen to the great lectures. You may think that you are in this environment out of your choice that is not true, it is his wish based on your karmas. So, what is expected out of you is that your work should be pure, your actions should help people, you should be humble, you should be approachable, and you should be devoting your duty to make his world more beautiful, truthful and trustworthy. People working with you should love you from the heart, should respect you from the heart. Your money spending decisions should be good for the people working with you and for the society.

If you are a rich person and have excess money, see how your money can gift food to the poor and needy, provide education to children or help starved people or elderly people. This is important to purify your money. Like you purify your body by washing, you purify your mind by good deeds and by chanting his holy name; you need to purify your money by regularly gifting a part of it to the more needy and more deserving ones. This is expected out of you. He gave us all the money and comfort; we can serve Him better by further gifting it to his people. You never know what is going to happen in the next birth if you are not doing your duty and sacrifice as per his prescribed system. In *kaliyuga*, jaap is very easy, one can do it alongwith doing other things, e.g. while bathing, travelling. There is no substitute of doing jaap.

If you are a household person or in a less busy job – then take on to meditation, take on to helping others wherever you can, go to places of worship, be soft spoken. Again your effort should be in beautifying his environment as per your capacity and reach. You have got into a different position again based on your karmas. One should always stay focused on God and keep doing one's assigned duty. This alone is enough for liberation – nothing else is needed for liberation if one is able to practise it.

When you start this journey and decide to purify your intellect that it does well to the people, you will find that it automatically purifies your heart. Heart and intelligence will purify your speech and then it will make you a sober and humble person. You started with a focus only on intelligence and you ended with a complete purity of everything in you. Purification process does not limit itself to one place, it spreads.

If you are not a very intelligent person and you took on to meditation, it will purify the heart; it will purify the whole system again. Two people started with a different focus but ended up with the same results. This result will take you to God – in this very birth if you are committed.

Every act is primarily driven by one's nature. Environment acts as catalyst which is earning of previous karmas. Nature means a combination of anger, ego, desire, likings, dislikings, etc. If you have the feelings of hatred, if you are hurting the feelings of others, if you are involved in acts of deceit, then despite your acts of attempt to meditation, giving alms, etc. will not yield the results important to start the journey towards God. Positive karmas being performed will just result in more comforts in return but God's way needs different qualities in individuals. So, one has to start purifying oneself if he is serious about the journey towards God's home.

This attempt once started, will slowly yield positive results. Nothing will happen overnight. You can't change your nature overnight; it needs serious dedication, attempt, sacrifice and time.

Lord says: In this world, there is no purifier as great as knowledge; he who has attained purity of heart through prolonged practice of karmayoga, automatically sees the light of Truth in the self in course of time.

इस संसारमें ज्ञानके समान पवित्र करनेवाला नि:संदेह कुछ भी नहीं है । उस ज्ञानको कितने ही कालसे कर्मयोगके द्वारा शुद्धान्त:करण हुआ मनुष्य अपने-आप ही आत्मामें पा लेता है ॥

Chapter 4 - verse 38

When you follow the path of self purification through various sacrifices (among sacrifices the highest sacrifice is chanting his holy name), then the purification brings the transcendental knowledge from within yourself from your soul. You will start getting the knowledge from within on what to do and how to do.

> Lord says: For, as the blazing fire reduces the fuel to ashes, Arjuna, even so the fire of Knowledge turns all actions to ashes.
>
> क्योंकि हे अर्जुन! जैसे प्रज्वलित अग्नि ईंधनोंको भस्ममय कर देता है, वैसे ही ज्ञानरूप अग्नि सम्पूर्ण कर्मोंको भस्ममय कर देता है॥
>
> Chapter 4 – verse 37

This message has a very deep meaning – more than as it appears in the sentences. It gives the importance of knowledge in scriptures like Bhagavad Gita. It has the power to burn the karmas but for that, the knowledge must bring in the change in the individual.

If the individual is committed and follows the scriptures and their embedded messages, then they can bring in a quick change in the individual and take him to the path towards God. They have the power of burning one's old bad karmas over a period. But if one is not sincere in his scriptures and does not follow their messages and does with his own whims, then even these scriptures are unable to do good to the individual.

When one reads scriptures, they will anyway leave their positive impact on an individual but one should not undo their positive effect with the negative karmas in parallel. For example – a business man, who goes to temple every day, offers food to the poor regularly and at the same time is also doing the business in an unfair means – then this error will wipe away the good results produced by the good karmas.

Next, he may not rise or may fall depending on what is more intense. So, people who are engaged in sattvika, rajasika and tamasika all the time just switching from one to another are lost in the system as they are not clear on where they wish to go and they come on heavy on the God's system. They keep ascending to heaven to enjoy fruits of good actions and returning on earth for the sufferings of their bad actions.

The power of internal purity

Man Changa to Kathauti Mein Ganga. All castes are same when it comes to internal purity. Internal purity makes you brahman in God's eyes.

Raidassji was a great saint. He lived in *Kashi*. He used to perfom the duty of a shoemaker/repairer and sit on the bank of *Ganges*. As we all know that Ganges is the purest river on earth. Lord Krishna has said that among rivers, I am Ganges. Ganges has the power of purifying and cleaning all sins of the people who take bath in Ganges. Hindus immerse the remains of all their near and dear ones in Ganges after death – something which is followed for no one knows for how many years.

There was also a very learned brahman in Kashi who used to do the last rites of the departed souls for the pilgrims to Ganges. He knew Raidassji as a shoemaker and not as a saint. Since they were living day and night on the same river banks – they knew each other quite well.

There are few auspicious days that are considered good for having bath in Ganges. On one such day, lot of people from the villages and cities came over to Ganges for a holy bath. Raidassji repaired the shoes free of charge on that day as he wanted to help the people who came for pilgrimage. Now the auspicious time was about to be over when a Panditji was rushing towards the Ganges as he had till then not taken the holy bath. He was busy performing a few religious rites for the pilgrims. Pilgrims normally give expensive gifts and cash to pandits.

So, as Panditji rushed towards the Ganges so that he could take bath before the auspicious time is over (as he understood the importance of auspicious times as written in scriptures when Sun, Moon and stars take a particular position in the galaxy) he saw Raidassji repairing the shoes and he asked him if he had taken the holy bath. Raidassji said no. So ne invited Raidassji to come along but Raidassji felt that if he did that, some of the people may have to go back home with torn shoes, so he decided not to go for the holy bath and stay back for work.

Auspicious time was over. Some people were still having a bath but most of the people returned to the banks and so did Panditji. Panditji looked very sad as he was gifted two large sized gold bangles by a devotee and those got swept in the river Ganges as he was having his bath as both the bangles were loose. Raidassji asked the reason of sadness from Panditji. Raidassji felt that was no reason to be sad and since he had very high regard for Panditji, he wanted to help him. So, he put his hands in Kathauti (a pot that shoemakers keep which is filled with water so that they can immerse the shoes in water and make them soft) and took out both the bangles that Panditji lost in the river while bathing and gave them to Panditji. *Man Changa* (If the mind is pure) *to Kathauti mein Ganga* (then Ganges is there with you).

That day Panditji realised the meaning of purity. Panditji was a deserving soul. He changed his path to go for salvation under the guidance of Raidassji.

To reach God one should meditate while performing all his duties

Power of meditation – It purifies you and you get God's love and support.

Lord Krishna has very clearly stated that a person engaged in meditation on God and doing all his duties without attachment reaches God as a rule defined by God.

Once the inner self is purified, then the mind will not wander around in different directions and will get focused on God. Once it gets focused on God, the journey towards God will start

God's meditation and rightful duty together will uplift you very fast to God's home. Meditation will help keep you on the right track. When you meditate, you get a pull from God as well. Meditation and chanting His holy name will ensure that your karmas do not go wrong.

When karmas go right, the only destination is God. Meditation also improves and cleanses your nature. Once your inner self is purified, you are entitled to liberation.

Lord says: Arjuna, he who with his mind disciplined through Yoga in the form of practice of meditation and thinking of nothing else, is constantly engaged in contemplation of God attains the supremely effulgent Divine Purusa (God).

हे पार्थ! यह नियम है कि परमेश्वरके ध्यानके अभ्यासरूप योगसे युक्त, दूसरी ओर न जानेवाले चित्तसे निरन्तर चिन्तन करता हुआ मनुष्य परम प्रकाशरूप दिव्य पुरुषको अर्थात् परमेश्वरको ही प्राप्त होता है॥

Chapter 8 - verse 8

> Lord says: He who departs from the body, thinking of Me alone even at the time of death, attains My state; there is no doubt about it.
>
> जो पुरुष अन्तकालमें भी मुझको ही स्मरण करता हुआ शरीरको त्याग कर जाता है, वह मेरे साक्षात् स्वरूपको प्राप्त होता है—इसमें कुछ भी संशय नहीं है॥
>
> Chapter 8 – verse 5

There is a secret in this, you will not remember him at the time of death unless you have been remembering him through the life.

> Arjuna, that eternal unmanifest supreme Purusa in whom all beings reside and by whom all this is pervaded, is attainable only through exclusive devotion.
>
> हे पार्थ! जिस परमात्माके अन्तर्गत सर्वभूत हैं और जिस सच्चिदानन्दघन परमात्मासे यह समस्त जगत् परिपूर्ण है, वह सनातन अव्यक्त परम पुरुष तो अनन्य भक्तिसे ही प्राप्त होने योग्य है॥
>
> Chapter 8 – verse 22

> Lord says: Whosoever offers Me with love a leaf, a flower, a fruit or water, I, appear in person before that selfless devotee of sinless mind, and delightfully partake of that article offered by him with love.
>
> जो कोई भक्त मेरे लिये प्रेमसे पत्र, पुष्प, फल, जल आदि अर्पण करता है, उस शुद्धबुद्धि निष्काम प्रेमी भक्तका प्रेमपूर्वक अर्पण किया हुआ वह पत्र-पुष्पादि मैं सगुणरूपसे प्रकट होकर प्रीतिसहित खाता हूँ॥
>
> Chapter 9 – verse26

People who worship Krishna and offer fruits, water, flowers and Tulsi to him, Lord says that I appear in person in front of the purified soul and eat the offering with love. Look at his greatness and humbleness.

One who runs the system and the universe comes running to eat your offered fruits – That is the power of love. God is very weak by heart and a little love is enough to pull him down in front of you. When you can get him down in front of you with a little love, do you really need support of any human being focused in the material system? He owns and runs the whole system, he is the source of all energy, and he is your final home. No one should waste energy in getting too deep in the material world.

You need money and house and other amenities to live. Bhagavad Gita says that you should live maintaining the world order; you do not need to leave anything. If you are a rich person, you do not need to leave your home and live in a smaller home or a forest but you need to change the environment of your home so that God is ready to come to your home.

He will come only when the environment of your home is clean – people love each other, people are humble and not greedy and selfish. You need to spend your money wisely to help the needy, poor and deserving in God's system. You do not need to leave anything but you also do not need to hoard amenities beyond your basic needs with sinful acts. If you have a skill, that skill is given by Him – then the earnings from that skill need to be used for purification.

Lot of rich people have very false ego. No one can share the experience on what happens to the individual at the time of death because the person who could have shared the experience is dead. Each one of us is going to face that moment of death. Scriptures say that the pain of dying is unbearable – physical and emotional. A person is going to lose everything that he has gathered all his life with lot of efforts in right or wrong ways. Only people who do not get disturbed are those who know they are going back to God's home and to His system – they are God loving people and know the destination after death. Love Him all the time, sacrifice as much as you can during the life and keep chanting His holy name for a beautiful journey after death.

Karmayoga and renunciation will take you to God's home

Work without attachment does wonders. It takes away the anger from you, it takes away the desire from you, and it takes away the ego from you. And it still makes you work and perform your duties. When you get rid of anger, ego and desire, you are always focused on God while performing your duties. When your focus is on God while performing your duties, you do your duties well because you have His support in performing your duties.

So, with a single change in you, you get everything including God. You get rid of anger, ego, and desire. You get His blessings and support and you do your duties well.

This practice brings in all peace within you and you become entitled to merge in God.

> Lord says: Therefore, go on efficiently doing your duty at all times without attachment. Doing work without attachment man attains the Supreme.
>
> इसलिये तू निरन्तर आसक्तिसे रहित होकर सदा कर्तव्यकर्मको भलीभाँति करता रह। क्योंकि आसक्तिसे रहित होकर कर्म करता हुआ मनुष्य परमात्माको प्राप्त हो जाता है॥
>
> Chapter 3 - verse 19

Knowledge is better than constantly attempting to reach God without knowledge.

Meditation and remembering God's face all the time is even superior to knowledge written in scriptures. Renunciation of all fruits of action is considered even superior to meditation as this brings in peace. Now here comes the play of God's Maya as well, so rightfully one who is seeking His blessings only will be able to achieve the renunciation.

> Lord says: Knowledge is better than practice without discernment, meditation on God is superior to knowledge, and renunciation of the fruit of actions is even superior to meditation; for, peace immediately follows renunciation.
>
> मर्मको न जानकर किये हुए अभ्याससे ज्ञान श्रेष्ठ है; ज्ञानसे मुझ परमेश्वरके स्वरूपका ध्यान श्रेष्ठ है और ध्यानसे भी सब कर्मोंके फलका त्याग श्रेष्ठ है; क्योंकि त्यागसे तत्काल ही परम शान्ति होती है॥
>
> Chapter 12 – verse 12

Renunciation is above everything. But renunciation will come only with His blessings and hence meditation is the enabler to get to renunciation. Renunciation is the last stage when the devotee is all set to reach him within this life.

Perform all actions keeping maintenance of the world order in mind

> Lord said: It is through action without attachment alone that Janaka and other wise men reached perfection. Having in view the maintenance of the world order too, you should take to action.
>
> जनकादि ज्ञानीजन भी आसक्तिरहित कर्मद्वारा ही परम सिद्धिको प्राप्त हुए थे। इसलिये तथा लोकसंग्रहको देखते हुए भी तू कर्म करनेको ही योग्य है अर्थात् तुझे कर्म करना ही उचित है॥
>
> Chapter 3 - verse 20

Lord has although advised actions without attachment to reach perfection which is reaching His home. In process of meeting this objective, one is advised to keep the maintenance of the world order as things will change from time to time while basic values will never change. So, if one is a rich person and is expected to keep a particular status and living, there is nothing wrong in that. It is just that you are keeping an eye on the maintenance of the world order and at the same time performing all your natural duties for the sake of sacrifice without attachment.

In fact, not following the maintenance of the world order will make one look out of the place with an intention to attract attention. A true devotee will never want to get into that position where he wants to get attention. Objective is sacrifice, objective is doing all duties without attachment, objective is to give back, objective is internal purification, objective is meditation and all this can be performed without compromising on the maintenance of the world order.

Worship of Lord Krishna is a complete worship

Sun provides us the light and energy. We will be no more without Sun. All fruits and vegetables draw their growth from moon and become full of taste and juices. Rivers and rains provide us water. Trees provide us fruits, vegetables and oxygen. Ayurvedic medicines get their medicinal properties from moonlight. The list of blessings is endless.

If we worship Krishna, it is a complete worship of all the Gods as He is a source of all the blessings through various sources. Hence Krishna worship is a complete worship. Everything has evolved from Lord Krishna and finally everything will merge in him.

All Gods and devtas draw their energy and purpose from Lord Krishna and fulfill their assigned duties and while fulfilling their duties, they work towards their way upwards to merge in Lord in due course of time. So, Lord Krishna has explained that how all these devtas are His creations only. Hence one can worship Lord Krishna and this worship is complete in all respects as there is nothing else but Krishna.

Lord says – I am the dearest friend. Yes, most of the people – Gopis, Prahlad, Meera loved Him more than they worshipped Him. Worshipping can have some hidden expectations – Love has no hidden expectations. Love is love and is pure. It will happen when you start following His path. His path is so beautiful that its beauty will overshadow all the material expectations. It happened to Meera, it happened to Gopis and it can happen to you.

It is only the wish to meet Him and a wish to reach Him. There is a state higher than that when that wish also goes away – when you are happy with single sided love – that moment there is no difference between God and a devotee or lover. This is called *Parabhakti*.

They are all the same. You can reach that stage by constant chanting of His holy name and by remembering Him all the time – love is remembering all the time and when that stage is reached, you will feel the lightness and you will understand what pleasure actually means and how different is it from this material world.

Source : www.bhagavad-gita.us

Worshipping decides different destinations

> Lord says: Those who are votaries of Gods, go to Gods, those who are votaries of manes, reach the manes; those who adore the spirits, reach the spirits and those who worship me come to Me alone. That is why My devotees are no longer subject to birth and death.
>
> देवताओंको पूजनेवाले देवताओंको प्राप्त होते हैं, पितरोंको पूजनेवाले पितरोंको प्राप्त होते हैं, भूतोंको पूजनेवाले भूतोंको प्राप्त होते हैं और मेरा पूजन करनेवाले भक्त मुझको ही प्राप्त होते हैं। इसलिये मेरे भक्तोंका पुनर्जन्म नहीं होता ॥
>
> Chapter 9 - verse 25

There are many worlds below God's Home and they are all governed by time. We have this world in which we live. There is heaven and astral world.

Various devtas sit in any of these worlds. If you worship them, then your aspiration is to reach them after death. Now that is an aspiration which may or may not get fulfilled as it depends on your current karmas but even if this does get fulfilled, then you only reach to their place as you defined that place as your destination and not God's home. From there you may again fall back on earth after enjoying the fruits of your good karmas.

If you stay focused on Krishna all the time, then your aspiration is to reach Him. Now if you show commitment and your karmas are also supportive, then you get his blessings and you cross over all other worlds to reach His abode which is all peace and beyond time, which should be your destination.

Krishna showed Vishnu form to Arjun

Section – 5

Failure is also success on His path

Shri Ram Darbar

Failure is also success on His path

Karmayogi who fails to reach God still meets with a very positive destiny and more positive environment to reach God in next birth. His devotion to God gets carried with him and he revives the divine consciousness in the next birth and with a better environment in next birth and previous devotion and commitment to reach God, he finds God in the next birth.

Failed but sincere efforts on God's path yields only a positive result.

Arjuna asked Lord Krishna as to what happens to the devotee who takes on to the path of self realisation and is also sincere in his efforts but fails to achieve the perfection as it is so difficult to win over the mind and the senses.

Lord says that no evil happens to the Devotee who has started journey of self realisation and he meets with only positive results.

> Sri Bhagavan said: Arjuna, there is no fall for him either here or hereafter. For, O My beloved, none who strives for self-redemption (i.e. God-realisation) ever meets with evil destiny.
>
> श्रीभगवान् बोले—हे पार्थ! उस पुरुषका न तो इस लोकमें नाश होता है और न परलोकमें ही। क्योंकि हे प्यारे! आत्मोद्धारके लिये अर्थात् भगवत्प्राप्तिके लिये कर्म करनेवाला कोई भी मनुष्य दुर्गतिको प्राप्त नहीं होता॥
>
> Chapter 6 – verse 40

Such a person who has strayed from Yoga, obtains the higher worlds (heaven, etc.) to which men of meritorious deeds alone are entitled, and having resided there for innumerable years, takes birth of pious and prosperous parents.

योगभ्रष्ट पुरुष पुण्यवानोंके लोकोंको अर्थात् स्वर्गादि उत्तम लोकोंको प्राप्त होकर, उनमें बहुत वर्षोंतक निवास करके फिर शुद्ध आचरणवाले श्रीमान् पुरुषोंके घरमें जन्म लेता है॥

Chapter 6 - verse 41

Or if he is possessed of dispassion, then not attaining to those regions he is born in the family of enlightened Yogis; but such a birth in this world is very difficult to obtain.

अथवा वैराग्यवान् पुरुष उन लोकोंमें न जाकर ज्ञानवान् योगियोंके ही कुलमें जन्म लेता है। परन्तु इस प्रकारका जो यह जन्म है, सो संसारमें निःसन्देह अत्यन्त दुर्लभ है॥

Chapter 6 - verse 42

Arjuna, he automatically regains in that birth the latencies of even-mindedness of his previous birth; and through that he strives harder than ever for perfection in the form of God-realisation.

वहाँ उस पहले शरीरमें संग्रह किये हुए बुद्धि-संयोगको अर्थात् समबुद्धिरूप योगके संस्कारोंको अनायास ही प्राप्त हो जाता है और हे कुरुनन्दन! उसके प्रभावसे वह फिर परमात्माकी प्राप्तिरूप सिद्धिके लिये पहलेसे भी बढ़कर प्रयत्न करता है॥

Chapter 6 - verse 43

> The other one who takes birth in a rich family, though under the sway of his senses, feels drawn towards God by force of the habit acquired in his previous birth; nay, even the seeker of Yoga (in the form of even - mindedness) transcends the fruit of actions performed with some interested motive as laid down in the Vedas.
>
> वह श्रीमानोंके घरमें जन्म लेनेवाला योगभ्रष्ट पराधीन हुआ भी उस पहलेके अभ्याससे ही निःसन्देह भगवान्‌की ओर आकर्षित किया जाता है, तथा समबुद्धिरूप योगका जिज्ञासु भी वेदमें कहे हुए सकाम कर्मोंके फलको उल्लंघन कर जाता है ॥
>
> Chapter 6 - verse 44

Karmayogi is one who performs all his prescribed duties and is also detached. He is focused on God and success and failure do not cause much change to his peace of mind. This is a practice that has to be performed to perfection, all this will not happen without effort and determination and by chanting His holy name.

Soul carries the burden of the old karmas. Old karmas are a mix of good and bad. If it is good, then your environment in which you live and your life is good and supportive for God-realisation. If you are carrying a higher burden of bad karmas, then the number of obstacles in your life will be more.

So, for a person who performs all his duties religiously, His previous karmas will act as friends or foes at each step making the life smoother or difficult. If you are determined, then you may get liberated in this very birth but if you fail (and you may fail due to many reasons – old karmas causing disturbance, unable to change the nature built over many births etc.), then you will meet with one of the following destinies:

Verse 41 – You may reach heaven; you may enjoy comfortable life over there for many years and after that take birth in a rich and pious family. Your strive for God realisation will naturally come to you as it travelled along with the soul, so you will start from there where you left earlier in the last birth on earth . (Your karmas in heaven do not count as that is a place of enjoyment rather than advancing the journey towards God's home and that is the reason that wise people call it a waste of time). Since one is attracted to God by birth, he strives harder to reach him.

Verse 42 – Second destiny for a failed Yogi (Vairagyavan) has the most beautiful journey. He does not go to heaven. He defeats the path to heaven and hence does not waste time in enjoying heavenly pleasures. He is immediately reborn in a family of religious, intellectual, pious, God realised and enlightened Yogis and continues his journey towards God's home. He carries the attraction towards God realisation from the previous birth and he also gets the right environment which helps him achieve the missed goal of God realisation. However such a birth is very rare and comes to only a few deserving people. This birth comes to the people who had advanced in the detachment and renunciation but failed somewhere in doing the perfection.

There is a major difference between the two. In the first one, there is journey to heaven and time spent there. Return on earth is in a rich family. Here the environment is good but not so promising for God realisation as the second one. One can notice that rich families do not always have peace. Within the family members, you may find some very pious people. They are souls progressing towards God realisation but are also attached to material activities. Also family circumstances may force and drift one towards more materialistic world despite the enlightenment that soul may have got due to previous births. Where as the other birth is very promising, it gives you the family environment that supports you towards achieving the goal for God realisation. This family has enough money to meet their basic needs, richness is in their environment, richness is in their thoughts and richness is in their deeds.

You can also create a heaven like environment on earth. If a family has enough money, you can create a highly comfortable life on earth as well. But does it help in God-realisation, answer is "No". When God dismisses the time spent in heaven where you can do no new karmas, it will not be wise to create a similar environment on earth where you are allowed to do new karmas. Time has to be spent on God's path and not in creating a dream world. Leading a good life is different to living a life with attraction to material richness.

It is easier for a committed Karmayogi to reach God

Yogi focused on Lord Krishna is supreme. You do not need to go in isolation or do extreme penances to reach Him. That is a very difficult route not to be adopted by a Karmayogi. Bhagavad Gita's teaching is that karmayogi reaches God faster than others and it is an easier way to reach God's home.

> Lord says: The Yogi is superior to ascetics; he is regarded superior even to those versed in sacred lore. The Yogi is also superior to those who perform action with some interested motive. Therefore Arjuna, do become a Yogi.
>
> योगी तपस्वियोंसे श्रेष्ठ है, शास्त्रज्ञानियोंसे भी श्रेष्ठ माना गया है और सकाम कर्म करनेवालोंसे भी योगी श्रेष्ठ है; इससे हे अर्जुन! तू योगी हो ॥
>
> Chapter 6 – verse 46

If one is performing all his duties and is also fully detached, sorrows and pleasures do not disturb him. He is a Yogi. Yogi is superior to those who are engaged in constant study of Vedas and religious books. Yogi is also superior to the people who are performing all duties but are bound and focused on results of their activities. They go through pleasures and pains in their transaction or in the path of their duties. They are also subjected to the birth and death cycle again – they transcend to heaven to enjoy the fruits of their good deeds and return to earth after their merits are exhausted.

So, Krishna advised Arjuna to become a Yogi. Here the expectation from Arjuna was to perform his duty of fighting the righteous war but not focused on the results or outcome of the war. In the same way expectation from individuals is to perform their natural duties with no focus on the positive or negative results as outcome of their duties. Focus on results also makes you very weak and fearful in your approach and fear is *tamasika*.

Krishna also recognised that among all the Yogis, the one who constantly meditates/chants holy name of Krishna is Supreme. When you are focused on Krishna, there are few very important differences that come up. Some of them are given below:

a. You are constantly being blessed by Lord as you meditate on Him and then it is His duty to take care of you.
b. If in the process, something goes wrong, nothing to worry; He will take care as that is His commitment. Just surrender to Lord Krishna.

> Lord says: Resigning all your duties to Me, the all-powerful and all supporting Lord, take refuge in Me alone; I shall absolve you of all sins, worry not.
>
> सम्पूर्ण धर्मोंको अर्थात् सम्पूर्ण कर्तव्यकर्मोंको मुझमें त्यागकर तू केवल एक मुझ सर्वशक्तिमान्, सर्वाधार परमेश्वरकी ही शरणमें आ जा। मैं तुझे सम्पूर्ण पापोंसे मुक्त कर दूँगा, तू शोक मत कर॥
>
> Chapter 18 - verse 66

c. You have fixed your mind on Krishna as your destination so your karmas will get purified.

If you do not surrender on to him, then you are bound by results of your actions. Good deeds result in reaping the good fruits. Bad deeds result in reaping the bad fruits.

Destiny (Latencies of past actions) – an important compelling influencer in your life

There are few incidents that happen in life which are pre-written and where you by compelling influence decide in their favour. Destiny will have both good and bad decisions. Destiny will not let you do wrong also where the things need to be in your favour. Destiny comes in few very important milestones of your life. You wrote this destiny yourself in your last birth according to your karmas and you are rewriting it for your next birth.

> Lord says: In the branch of learning known as Sankhya, which prescribes means for neutralising all actions, the five factors have been mentioned as contributory to the accomplishment of all actions; know them all from me Arjuna.
>
> The following are the factors operating towards the accomplishment of actions, viz., the body and the doer, the organs of different kinds and the different functions of manifold kinds; and the fifth is Daiva, latencies of past actions.
>
> हे महाबाहो! सम्पूर्ण कर्मोंकी सिद्धिके ये पाँच हेतु कर्मोंका अन्त करनेके लिये उपाय बतलानेवाले सांख्यशास्त्रमें कहे गये हैं, उनको तू मुझसे भलीभाँति जान॥
>
> इस विषयमें अर्थात् कर्मोंकी सिद्धिमें अधिष्ठान और कर्ता तथा भिन्न-भिन्न प्रकारके करण एवं नाना प्रकारकी अलग-अलग चेष्टाएँ और वैसे ही पाँचवाँ हेतु दैव है॥
>
> Chapter 18 - verse 13, 14

Krishna towards the end of the Bhagavad Gita explained the role of destiny very beautifully. Now Lord Krishna wanted to tell that there are certain decisions which are not in your hand even while you are free to perform your karmas the way you wish to. Krishna had earlier explained that he does not decide your karmas but these are decided by yourself. And still there are karmas that are performed by you without a conscious decision by you in this life. You cannot take a decision against destiny even when you are free to take a decision in life.

Krishna told Arjuna that now you can decide to fight or not to fight. But he said that there is a reason that you cannot decide against the fight. Because that is the destiny. This destiny will have a compelling influence on you and will drive you to fight. This destiny is written by none else other than you. Here with this destiny, you are doing God's work as this is also God's will so you have support from his system to win as you are fighting for the right cause.

In everyone's life, there are few destinies which bring in strong influence on you to take the decision. These could be right or wrong decisions, but these are influenced by your destiny (Latencies of past actions). These right or wrong decisions influenced by destiny are nothing else but the previous karmas. Destiny incidents are like accidents, marriage, early deaths, handicaps, diseases, old age sufferings, relationship sufferings, limited earnings despite hard work. These are prewritten and not so easy to change. One in thousands committed on the path of God realisation can change the destiny.

Markandeya Rishi had the destiny of early death during the childhood. He worshipped Lord *Shiva* with love and devotion. Lord Shiva blessed him for a long life and Markandeya Rishi wrote many scriptures in service of God. Destiny can be changed but that needs lot of love and devotion from you towards God. Markandeya Rishi changed his destiny of dying at the age of 16.

So, while one has no control on the destiny, one can always take shelter under God all the time. This shelter will shield one from the results of the karmas performed under destiny. So, assuming you have a destiny that drives you to do an error. This error (whatever be the nature) becomes your fresh karma and will write your future destiny. Even while you had no control on the karma performed under destiny decisions in this birth, yet you are not free from the bindings or results of that karma. But if you take shelter under him and surrender the results of all actions on to him, then this karma performed under destiny does not yield any fresh karma – good or bad .

Remember both good and bad karmas are nothing but a binding. Bad karmas result in bad destiny and good karmas result in good destiny which could be heaven or a superior birth. Only way to come out of the birth and death cycles is in-action which is not practical so the only way is to surrender all actions on to Him. If one understands this in life, it can bring in a big change.

Actions driven by ego should not be confused as destiny

It was discussed that ego is one of the five drivers of actions by individuals. Many actions that one may attribute to destiny may not be right; these may have been driven by one's ego. Ego is very powerful. Ego wants to stand in front everywhere – good acts and bad acts. Ego makes one feel proud of even bad actions that one has performed.

You need to watch this most powerful enemy, i.e. ego. It can ruin one's journey and destination. It will not come under control by sheer determination because if it is there, it will pop up whenever it sees the opportunity. One has to follow various recommendations listed in the scriptures to control the ego.

Also, one has to leave the actions and thoughts of the material things. Material things are with individuals till the death and do not carry forward to the next birth, so your focus needs to be on the things that will carry forward to the next birth.

You can also see that ego, anger, desire travel with soul to the next birth from the fact that these never get old. Body gets old because it has completed its journey and is about to give way and die.

But ego, anger and desire is not destined for death that is why these do not get old. You will see the ego, desire and anger going strong with the individuals close to their death while their bodies have given their way.

Maya is always pulling you towards material world, only God's blessings will help

God is present in everyone. He is watching each and every action of ours. He is recording every action. According to one's karmas, God is making the appropriate environment available to the individuals. It is not so easy to come out of this Maya which is basically illusion of material things which is not real and is of no value to the individual after his death. After the death, what matters is only your karmas that you performed for which God (your own soul) is the witness. Soul stays untouched and is always pure. What suffers is your body based on your karmas.

Only way to come out of this Maya is to go to the source of Maya which is God. Surrender yourself on to him and keep chanting his holy name; he will take you out of this grip of Maya. Once Maya's impact gets reduced your vision of the path towards God will be much clearer.

This is what is also advised in Bhagavad Gita as below.

> Lord says: Arjuna, God abides in the heart of all creatures, causing them to revolve according to their Karma by His illusive power (Maya) as though mounted on a machine.
>
> हे अर्जुन! शरीररूप यन्त्रमें आरूढ़ हुए सम्पूर्ण प्राणियोंको अन्तर्यामी परमेश्वर अपनी मायासे उनके कर्मोंके अनुसार भ्रमण कराता हुआ सब प्राणियोंके हृदयमें स्थित है॥
>
> Chapter 18 - verse 61

Lord says : Take refuge in Him alone with all your being, Arjuna. By His mere grace you will attain supreme peace and the eternal abode.

हे भारत! तू सब प्रकारसे उस परमेश्वरकी ही शरणमें जा। उस परमात्माकी कृपासे ही तू परम शान्तिको तथा सनातन परमधामको प्राप्त होगा॥

Chapter 18 – verse 62

Sattvika and renunciation together help in liberation

Here it is clearly stated that good karmas and bad karmas – both produce bindings. To reach God, one has to renounce the fruits of all actions and you can do that only by meditating on Him all the time and surrendering all actions on to Him.

Along with renunciation, sattvika habits have to be followed. Rajasika and tamasika can never lead to liberation. So, one must get sattvika, do meditation (chant His holy name) and observe renunciation of fruits of all actions.

> Lord says: Agreeable, disagreeable and mixed – threefold, indeed, is the fruit that accrues after death from the actions of the unrenouncing. But there is none whatsoever for those who have renounced.
>
> कर्मफलका त्याग न करनेवाले मनुष्योंके कर्मोंका तो अच्छा-बुरा और मिला हुआ ऐसे तीन प्रकारका फल मरनेके पश्चात् अवश्य होता है, किन्तु कर्मफलका त्याग कर देनेवाले मनुष्योंके कर्मोंका फल किसी कालमें भी नहीं होता ॥
>
> Chapter 18 - verse 12

Lord says: A person in Krishna consciousness or in the mode of goodness does not hate anyone or anything which troubles his body. He performs his duties in the proper place and at the proper time without fearing the troublesome effects of his duty. Such a person situated in transcendence should be understood to be most intelligent and beyond all doubts in his activities.

General qualities of a devotee entitled to merge with God

Starting journey on His path is important.

Your food habits have a great impact on your nature. If you eat fruits, juices, natural vegetables, etc. You can have a longer life. These food habits help you tame your nature in a sattvika direction. These are sattvika foods.

If your food items are hot, pungent, spicy – these cause irritation and promote the feelings of anger and jealousy. This is rajasika food. If your food is overripe, unhygienic, unnatural for human beings to eat, then the food is tamasika and it takes you to the direction of lower worlds.

Everything that you do, you think, you eat can be categorised in sattvika, rajasika and tamasika. Sattvika promotes sattvika. Rajasika promotes rajasika, tamasika promotes tamasika. Also sattvika wants to dominate rajasika and tamasika. Rajasika wants to dominate sattvika and tamasika. Tamasika wants to dominate rajasika and sattvika.

If your food habits are tamasika and you are trying to follow a sattvika path through your intelligence, it will struggle and fall down on the way. It will not reach there. You will have to give up the tamasika food if you want to go down to the sattvika route.

Same goes the other way also – If you have adopted sattvika habits – food, thoughts, talks, actions and you want to now hurt someone – you will struggle as sattvika will dominate on you and will not let you do any error, you will have to go to tamasika habits to lead a regretful life.

One may think that I can adopt few sattvika habits but not all. Where will it lead me to? Well – It will lead one to a good living and a constant journey between heaven and earth and repeated birth and death cycles.

Now once you adopt sattvika habits, does it mean that you get liberated? No. Because the reward of good deeds will come to you by way of ascending to heaven after death and returning back to earth after the reward is exhausted.

So you will have to surrender the fruits of all your actions to God and that is the only way to avoid this up and down journey.

Surrender on to Him, adopt sattvika habits and see Him as the doer in everything. This way you will surpass all the fruits of good deeds and also surpass some of the bad deeds performed out of ignorance.

Lord says : Endowed with a pure intellect and partaking of a light, sattvika and regulated diet, living in a lonely and undefiled place, having rejected sound and other objects of sense, having controlled the mind, speech and body by restraining the mind and senses through firmness of a sattvika type, taking a resolute stand on dispassion, after having completely got rid of attraction and aversion and remaining ever devoted to the Yoga of meditation, having given up egotism, violence, arrogance, lust, anger and luxuries, devoid of the feeling of meum and tranquil of heart – such a man becomes qualified for oneness with Brahma, who is Truth, Consciousness and Bliss.

विशुद्ध बुद्धिसे युक्त तथा हलका, सात्त्विक और नियमित भोजन करनेवाला, शब्दादि विषयोंका त्याग करके एकान्त और शुद्ध देशका सेवन करनेवाला, सात्त्विक धारणशक्तिके द्वारा अन्तःकरण और इन्द्रियोंका संयम करके मन, वाणी और शरीरको वशमें कर लेनेवाला, राग-द्वेषको सर्वथा नष्ट करके भलीभाँति दृढ़ वैराग्यका आश्रय लेनेवाला तथा अहंकार, बल, घमण्ड, काम, क्रोध और परिग्रहका त्याग करके निरन्तर ध्यानयोगके परायण रहनेवाला, ममतारहित और शान्तियुक्त पुरुष सच्चिदानन्दघन ब्रह्ममें अभिन्नभावसे स्थित होनेका पात्र होता है ॥

Chapter 18 – verse 51-53

God loves one who neither hurts nor gets hurt

Not hurting is easy. Not getting hurt requires lot of meditation and spiritual advancement.

> Lord says: He who is not a source of annoyance to his fellow – creatures, and who in his turn does not feel vexed with his fellow – creatures, and who is free from delight and envy, perturbation and fear, is dear to Me.
>
> जिससे कोई भी जीव उद्वेगको प्राप्त नहीं होता और जो स्वयं भी किसी जीवसे उद्वेगको प्राप्त नहीं होता; तथा जो हर्ष, अमर्ष, भय और उद्वेगादिसे रहित है—वह भक्त मुझको प्रिय है ॥
>
> Chapter 12 - verse 15

Lord says that an individual who does not hurt or put some one in difficulty and also does not get hurt by anyone is dear to me. Not getting hurt will happen when you will see God in everyone, when you will see the truth, when you will know that if some one hurts you, he cannot disturb your peace of mind and he cannot take away your continuous attention and meditation on God.

He understands that breaths are not to be wasted in thinking of these silly things but breaths are better spent in chanting the Holy name and in remembering His blessings on us as He gave us the most beautiful creation of His, which is human birth and an opportunity for liberation. You cannot trade this opportunity of time in hurting someone or getting hurt by someone.

Jaap yagya is supreme yagya for liberation

Gayatri Mantra and *Hare Krishna Maha Mantra* – Way for God Realisation. There is no difference between Krishna and OM.

Lord Krishna says – Among various yagyas, I am Jaapyagya. This shows that Jaapyagya is above all the yagyas. Hence we should meditate chanting his holy name and *mantras*. Among Mahamantras – two Mantras have a specific mention – Gayatri Mantra in Bhagavad Gita and Hare Krishna Mantra. These mantras help connect intelligence with mind, help get God's blessings, help in purification, help in putting the individuals to the right path for God realisation.

Worshipping OM is a complete worship as it finds a great mention in Bhagavad Gita.

> Lord says: Among the great seers, I am *Bhrgu*; among words, I am the sacred syllable *OM*; among sacrifices, I am the sacrifice of Japa (muttering of sacred formulas); and among the immovables , the Himalayas
>
> मैं महर्षियोंमें भृगु और शब्दोंमें एक अक्षर अर्थात् ओंकार हूँ। सब प्रकारके यज्ञोंमें जपयज्ञ और स्थिर रहनेवालोंमें हिमालय पहाड़ हूँ॥
>
> Chapter 10 - verse 25

When you chant God's holy name, sattvika dominates on you at least for the duration of chanting the name. It will also leave an impact for a while. If you regularly chant God's mantras, then sattvika will start dominating on you for a greater duration of the time. Sattvika will bring in the desired purification.

Slowly one becomes fully purified and sattvika domination at the time of death takes one to higher worlds and it may lead one to God's home. So, nothing better than chanting his holy name and mantras.

Try chanting his holy name for at least 15 minutes in a day (which is just 1% of your time of a day) to start with and notice the difference yourself. You will soon increase the duration as it will bring a very pleasant change to your attitude, vision, humbleness and your overall life.

Krishna consciousness is not an artificial imposition on your mind, His name is the original energy of the living entity. When we hear His holy name and transcendental vibration—this consciousness is revived.

Worshipping OM

Lord says: Therefore, acts of sacrifice, charity and austerity, as enjoined by sacred precepts, are always commenced by noble persons, used to recitation of Vedic chants, with the invocation of the divine name 'OM'

इसलिये वेद-मन्त्रोंका उच्चारण करनेवाले श्रेष्ठ पुरुषोंकी शास्त्रविधिसे नियत यज्ञ, दान और तपरूप क्रियाएँ सदा इस परमात्माके नामको उच्चारण करके ही आरम्भ होती हैं॥

Chapter 17 – verse 24

Hari is Lord Krishna's pious name. Chanting Hari Naam washes off all the sins. Hari Naam has the power like OM for getting one rid of the bad old karmas and sins and to bring in the purification.

All sacrifices take you closer to God

Without sacrifice, you can never live happily here now or there after death.

Everything belongs to God. This world is created by Him. You are His creation. Whatever you get, you get from Him.

Sacrifice is the root of liberation. Sacrifice makes you pure. When you share your earnings with poor who are deserving people, your wealth becomes pure.

When you offer food to God and offer food to His deserving people (Ann Daan), you perform sacrifice that is accepted by lords. When you meditate – your mind and intelligence become pure.

Lord says : Some perform sacrifice with material possessions; some offer sacrifice in the shape of austerities; others sacrifice through the practice of Yoga; while some striving souls, observing austere vows, perform sacrifice in the shape of wisdom through the study of sacred texts.

कई पुरुष द्रव्यसम्बन्धी यज्ञ करनेवाले हैं, कितने ही तपस्यारूप यज्ञ करनेवाले हैं तथा दूसरे कितने ही योगरूप यज्ञ करनेवाले हैं, कितने ही अहिंसादि तीक्ष्ण व्रतोंसे युक्त यत्नशील पुरुष स्वाध्यायरूप ज्ञानयज्ञ करनेवाले हैं ॥

Chapter 4 - verse 28

Lord says: Arjuna, Yogis who enjoy the nectar that has been left over after the performance of a sacrifice attain the eternal Brahma. To the man who does not offer sacrifice, even this world is not happy; how, then, can the other world be happy?

हे कुरुश्रेष्ठ अर्जुन! यज्ञसे बचे हुए अमृतका अनुभव करनेवाले योगीजन सनातन परब्रह्म परमात्माको प्राप्त होते हैं। और यज्ञ न करनेवाले पुरुषके लिये तो यह मनुष्यलोक भी सुखदायक नहीं है, फिर परलोक कैसे सुखदायक हो सकता है?॥

Chapter 4 - verse 31

Lord says: The virtuous who partake of what is left over after sacrifice, are absolved of all sins. Those sinful ones who cook for the sake of nourishing there bodies alone, partake of sin only.

यज्ञसे बचे हुए अन्नको खानेवाले श्रेष्ठ पुरुष सब पापोंसे मुक्त हो जाते हैं और जो पापीलोग अपना शरीर-पोषण करनेके लिये ही अन्न पकाते हैं, वे तो पापको ही खाते हैं॥

Chapter 3 - verse 13

Lord has stated that people who do not do sacrifice live a sinful life and they can never live happily now or die peacefully. Also as mentioned in Chapter 9, verse 16 of Bhagavad Gita, Lord says, "I am the sacrifice". So God has identified Himself as the sacrifice.

All actions except sacrifice bind you.....also follow give back

> Man is bound by his own action except when it is performed for the sake of sacrifice. Therefore, Arjuna, do you efficiently perform your duty, free from attachment, for the sake of sacrifice alone.
>
> यज्ञके निमित्त किये जानेवाले कर्मोंसे अतिरिक्त दूसरे कर्मोंमें लगा हुआ ही यह मनुष्यसमुदाय कर्मोंसे बँधता है । इसलिये हे अर्जुन ! तू आसक्तिसे रहित होकर उस यज्ञके निमित्त ही भलीभाँति कर्तव्यकर्म कर ॥
>
> Chapter 3 - verse 9

Actions without sacrifice are actions for the self. All actions for the self are binding in nature. Good actions, bad actions will all make one wander between heaven and hell.

One has to get rid of binding of all actions to reach His home, so one has to adapt the spirit of sacrifice. Sacrifice does not bind you, so **all** actions (natural duties) should be performed for the sake of **sacrifice** alone.

> Fostered by sacrifice, the Gods will surely bestow on you unasked all the desired enjoyments. He who enjoys the gifts bestowed by them without offering their share to them, is undoubtedly a thief.
>
> यज्ञके द्वारा बढ़ाये हुए देवता तुमलोगोंको बिना माँगे ही इच्छित भोग निश्चय ही देते रहेंगे। इस प्रकार उन देवताओंके द्वारा दिये हुए भोगोंको जो पुरुष उनको बिना दिये स्वयं भोगता है, वह चोर ही है॥
>
> Chapter 3 - verse 12

When you perform sacrifice through yagyas for the devtas, they not only fulfill your basic necessities but also give you more than what you need. All that one got in life is just because of the blessings of the Gods. One has to perform further sacrifices which is like giving it back to God, who gave you all these things.

When you get more than what you need, you got to recognise the blessings you have from Gods and it is your duty to perform further sacrifices and these sacrifices and the spirit of these sacrifices will take you closer to him.

Samatava Yoga – evenness of mind in success and failure–way to God

Samatava Yoga is feeling all the way same through the life and not to get disturbed with failures or enjoy the successes or Evenness of mind. What is going to happen is determined by your karmas and that is going to happen. So, one should spend all his time in dutiful karmas and meditation. Samatava Yoga is renunciation. Renunciation leads to peace. Renunciation in God's eyes is even above meditation. After renunciation, your next destination is God's home.

> Lord says: Endowed with equanimity, one sheds in this life both good and evil. Therefore, strive for the practice of this Yoga of equanimity. Skill in action lies in the practice of this Yoga.
>
> समबुद्धियुक्त पुरुष पुण्य और पाप दोनोंको इसी लोकमें त्याग देता है अर्थात् उनसे मुक्त हो जाता है। इससे तू समत्वरूप योगमें लग जा; यह समत्वरूप योग ही कर्मोंमें कुशलता है अर्थात् कर्मबन्धनसे छूटनेका उपाय है॥
>
> For, wise men possessing equipoised mind, renouncing the fruit of actions and freed from the shackles of birth, attain the blissful supreme state.
>
> क्योंकि समबुद्धिसे युक्त ज्ञानीजन कर्मोंसे उत्पन्न होनेवाले फलको त्यागकर जन्मरूप बन्धनसे मुक्त हो निर्विकार परमपदको प्राप्त हो जाते हैं॥
>
> Chapter 2 – verse 50-51

One's biggest enemy and one's best friend is one himself

Giving up desires is very important for going on to God's path. Righteous act, humbleness, sattvika habits and evenness of mind in success and failure should be observed. One must win over the senses and the mind. If this does not happen, then one will be lost. Only wishing to conquer the senses and mind will not yield results. For this one has to take to Yoga Yoga of meditation, Karmayoga will all help in conquering the lower self. Just a decision alone will not succeed; God's blessings has to come in for help and that will come following sattvika habits and by chanting his holy name.

> Lord says: One's own self is the friend of the soul by whom the lower self (consisting of the mind, senses and body) has been conquered; even so, the very Self of him, who has not conquered his lower self, behaves antagonistically like an enemy.
>
> परन्तु हे अर्जुन! कर्मयोगके बिना संन्यास अर्थात् मन, इन्द्रिय और शरीरद्वारा होनेवाले सम्पूर्ण कर्मोंमें कर्तापनका त्याग प्राप्त होना कठिन है और भगवत्स्वरूपको मनन करनेवाला कर्मयोगी परब्रह्म परमात्माको शीघ्र ही प्राप्त हो जाता है॥
>
> Chapter 6 – verse 6

God will step in to help you if you fail to invoke the inner self

On path of meditation, if one fails to invoke the inner self but one is loving and sincere in his effort, then God will step in to help achieve the truth and reach Him. Jaap alone will finally help you reach the Supreme.

Human life is too short. If one thinks sincerely, time goes so fast and this life may be over before one has the realisation of the truth. His Maya is very strong and will pull you towards all material activities.

You can overcome His Maya only with His blessings and His blessings will come only with love and meditation.

Since the life is short, one may not be able to overcome all the obstacles that disturb the peace and hence may not be able to reach Him but lord says that if your efforts are sincere and loving, then I will help you get to the truth by which you will reach me.

Lord says: On those ever united through meditation with Me and worshipping Me with love, I confer that Yoga of wisdom by which they come to me.

उन निरन्तर मेरे ध्यान आदिमें लगे हुए और प्रेमपूर्वक भजनेवाले भक्तोंको मैं वह तत्त्वज्ञानरूप योग देता हूँ, जिससे वे मुझको ही प्राप्त होते हैं ॥

Chapter 10 - verse 10

Lord says: To those who are constantly devoted and worship Me with love, I give the understanding by which they can come to me. In order to bestow My compassion on them, I, dwelling in their hearts, dispel their darkness born of ignorance by the illuminating lamp of knowledge.

हे अर्जुन! उनके ऊपर अनुग्रह करनेके लिये उनके अन्तःकरणमें स्थित हुआ मैं स्वयं ही उनके अज्ञानजनित अन्धकारको प्रकाशमय तत्त्वज्ञानरूप दीपकके द्वारा नष्ट कर देता हूँ॥

Chapter 10 - verse 11

True knowledge is seeing Him in everything

> In this world there is no purifier as great as Knowledge; he who has attained purity of heart through prolonged practice of KarmaYoga, automatically sees the light of truth in the self in course of time.
>
> इस संसारमें ज्ञानके समान पवित्र करनेवाला नि:संदेह कुछ भी नहीं है। उस ज्ञानको कितने ही कालसे कर्मयोगके द्वारा शुद्धान्त:करण हुआ मनुष्य अपने-आप ही आत्मामें पा लेता है॥
>
> Chapter 4 - verse 38

Through the reading of Bhagavad Gita, one comes across number of times on the true knowledge. Knowledge is attained through purification with karmayoga. Also it is not a very quick journey as it is mentioned that it is through prolonged practise of karmayoga that this knowledge is obtained.

But what is that knowledge. That knowledge which one attains through purification is nothing but seeing him everywhere and in everything. Nothing exists but He. Nothing was there but He. Nothing will be there but He. So the only goal worth pursuing in life is nothing but He (God).

Wishing all the readers a successful and a blessed spiritual journey.

Gayatri Mantra

ॐ भूर्भुवः स्वः तत्सवितुर्वरेण्यं
भर्गो देवस्य धीमहि धियो योनः प्रचोदयात्।

"Om Bhur Bhuvah Svaha tat Savitur Varenyam
Bhargo Devasya Dhimahi Dhiyo Yonah Prachodayat"

Oh Creator of the Universe! We meditate upon thy supreme splendor.
May thy radiant power illuminate our intellects,
Destroy our sins, and guide us in the right direction!

Lord says: Likewise, among the Srutis that can be sung, I am the variety known as Brhatsama; while among the Vedic hymns, I am the hymn known as Gayatri. Again, among the twelve months of the Hindu calendar, I am the month known as Margasirsa (corresponding approximately to Nov-Dec); and among the six seasons (successively appearing in India in the course of a year), I am the spring season.

तथा गायन करनेयोग्य श्रुतियोंमें मैं बृहत्साम और छन्दोंमें गायत्री छन्द हूँ तथा महीनोंमें मार्गशीर्ष और ऋतुओंमें वसन्त मैं हूँ॥

Chapter 10 - verse 35

Hare Krishna Mahamantra

**Hare Krishna, Hare Krishna, Krishna Krishna Hare Hare
Hare Rama , Hare Rama , Rama Rama Hare Hare**

Sri Radha – Krishna

Lord Ram, Sita, Laxman and Hanuman

Ekadshi Fast – **Fast for Krishna**

Goddess power is source of power in Gods. Ekadshi fast is observed by Krishna Devotees. Ekadshi fast leads one to liberation.

The story of Ekadshi fast is as follows. Lord *Vishnu* (Krishna) fought with a demon for many years. Demon was too strong. God could not kill him. So, God decided to take some rest before resuming fight. Lord Vishnu went to sleep. The demon saw the Lord sleeping and decided to attack him while he was sleeping. As soon as he lifted his weapon to attack, a Goddess emerged out of Lord Vishnu (Krishna) and started the fight with the demon. In no time, Goddess killed the demon. When lord woke up from his sleep, he found the demon was dead and a Goddess was standing on one side with folded hands out of grace to Lord Vishnu. Lord asked the Goddess – who killed this demon. Goddess answered that she killed the demon as he was about to attack the Lord in sleep. Lord thanked her that while he could not kill the demon, she had helped in killing him. Lord further asked – who you are and from where have you come. Goddess said – I am your power and have emerged out of your body.

That day was a Ekadshi Day (Ekadshi is the 11th day when the moon is rising and 11th day when the moon starts diminishing – it comes after every 14 days approximately). God told the Goddess that this date will be the most beloved date for me and people who fast on this day will get liberated.

Since that day, Ekadshi fast is observed by Krishna followers. Ekadshi comes every 14-15 days. Lord himself did not know all his powers – it is the Shakti and Goddess power in God that helps from time to time when God's need them the most.

Goddesses have appeared in person on many occasions to help when the Gods were in a difficult position to eradicate the evil powers. Mahalaxmi, Mahakali and Mahasaraswati are three powers behind the whole creation.

Goddesses are worshipped in many forms but they are all one Power – Call it Durga or Mahalaxmi or Radha. They all are one.

Gokul - 84 *khamba* and cows of Nand Baba

Lord Krishna was born 5100 years ago. On the night of his birth, Vasudevaji took him to Nand Village where Nand exchanged his daughter with Lord Krishna. Daughter of Nand and *Yashoda* was Goddess Durga. The place where Krishna spent his first seven years is called 84 Khamba and is located in Vrindavan, near Delhi. One can go and see the home which is still there. Lord Krishna had immense love for cows and he played with cows all his childhood. Cow is worshipped by devotees of Lord Krishna and people feed cows regularly in many places of India before they take their own meal. Cow is considered to be very pious by Hindus.

Lord Krishna with a Cow

Goddess Durga

Power of Mahalaxmi, Mahakali and Maha Saraswati. Durga's Temple - Vaishno Devi is in *Katra* – Jammu.

Goddesss Mahalaxmi is creation of all Gods and worlds

Radha is consort of Lord Krishna

They are worshipped together as Radha-Krishna.

Tulsi is worshipped in every Hindu family

Tulsi is worshipped in all temples. Blessings of Tulsi can wash all the sins. Ganga and Tulsi are symbols of ultimate purity and sacrifice.

Tulsi is offered to Lord Krishna. Tulsi is considered to be the purest and an example of great sacrifice. Vrindavan is also named on Tulsi (whose original name was Vrinda). Hindu homes have Tulsi plant in their garden and light a *diya* under Tulsi in the night. Tulsi saves you from all the bad omen at home. When *Prasadam* is offered to Lord Krishna, it is offered along with a Tulsi leaf, only then the Lord accepts it. Also by placing a Tulsi leaf on the prasadam – it gets completely purified even if there was some shortcomings in preparing it.

Tulsi plant at home should be watered every day. There is a story that Krishna's wife wanted to make donation equal to the weight of Lord Krishna to Narada Muni. On one side of the weighing scale a huge pile of gold was put and Lord Krishna sat on the other side. But gold could not lift Lord Krishna despite huge pile of gold on the scale. Then Narada Muniji suggested removing all the Gold and he placed a single leaf of Tulsi on one side and Lord Krishna got lifted. Tulsi carries such a respect and devotion in Lord Krishna's heart that he allowed himself to get lifted with a single Tulsi leaf. One must worship Tulsi for purity and blessing from both Tulsi and Lord Krishna.

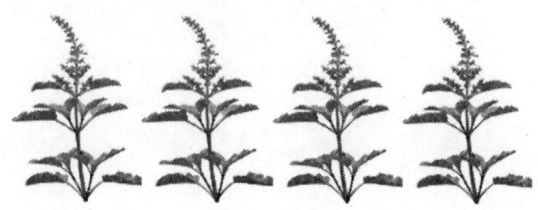

Glossary

- Arjuna – Principle warrior in Mahabharta who was taught Bhagavad Gita by Lord Krishna
- Avatar – Incarnation of God
- Adhikari – a deserving person
- Amritvani – Prayer for Lord Rama
- Astral World – Higher world
- Badrinath – Holy place in North India
- Brahman – Saint
- Bhakti – Meditation
- BhaktiYoga – Yoga of worshipping
- Bhaj – Chanting the Holy Name
- Bhrgu – Name of a saint
- Chetna – Consciousness. Consciousness in us is because of the Soul
- Daiva – Latencies of past actions
- Devotee – One who worships God
- Devtas – Devotees of Lord in higher worlds who bless humans
- Devlok – Home for higher souls closer to God
- Dalhousie – A hill station in India
- Darshan – Appearance
- Diya – Candle
- Guru – Teacher, Spiritual master/mentor
- Gunas – Inherent qualities of an individual
- Gopis – Female devotees of Lord Krishna who took birth in Vrindavan
- Ganges – Holy river in North India. It is considered the symbol of purity and is revered by all the Hindus. Its water is never contaminated even if it is kept for many years

- Ekadshi – 11th day in the Hindu Calender. Krishna's followers observe fast on this day
- Himalayas – Mountain ranges in India
- Havan – Offerings to Lords in sacrificial fire
- Jagdeesh Temple – Lord Vishnu Temple in Udaipur (India). Idol of Krishna that Meera worshipped is also there
- Jaap – Chanting Holy name of Lord
- Jivatma – Soul
- Karmas – One's actions in life
- Kurukshetra – A place in India, near Delhi where battle of Mahabharta was fought
- Katra (Jammu) – Temple of Vaishno Devi is in Katra (Jammu), India
- Karmayoga –Skill in Action through sacrifice and surrender to God
- Kalaatit – Above time.
- Kaal Kandoli – A place near Jammu (India) where Goddess Durga appeared and spent 12 years .
- Krishnalok – Home for Lord Krishna where time does not exist
- Kaliyuga – Present time period is Kaliyuga
- Kashi – A Holy city in India. Also called Varanasi
- Khamba – Pillars
- Kunti – Mother of Arjuna
- Liberation – Merging of Soul with the Oversoul
- Markandeya – Name of a Saint
- Maya – Attraction to the Material World
- Meera – Rajput princess and devotee of Lord Krishna
- Mantras – Shlokas/verses in praise of God
- Narada – Saint and devotee of Lord Krishna
- Nand Baba – Father of Sri Krishna
- OM – God is identified with this syllable. OM means complete God

- Pandavas – Five sons of Pandu. They faught Mahabharata with Kauravas, their cousins
- Prahlad – Son of a demon king and a great devotee of Lord Krishna
- Partha – Krishna addressed Arjun as Partha
- Paramdham – God's Home. Final Destination
- Parbrahm – Oversoul
- Pitrlok – Higher World where souls of ancestors reside
- Parabhakti – Highest state of meditation
- Prakrti – Nature
- Prasadam – Food taken by devotees after offering to God
- Rajasika – Person attracted to material world. Mode of Passion
- राम – Lord Rama
- Ram Sharnam – An organisation of devotees of Lord Rama
- Rishi – Saint
- Rishikesh – Holy town in north India
- Radha – Consort of Lord Krishna
- Radhalok – God's home
- Sankhyayoga – Path of knowledge
- Sattvika – Truthful and Saintly, Pure Hearted. Mode of Goodness
- Shlokas – Verses
- Soul – Atma. God's presence in us that keeps us alive. Departure of Soul leaves one dead
- Shiva – Hindu God
- Saligrama – Lord Krishna is also worshipped as Saligrama, the rounded black stones found in river Narmada
- Sanskar – Moral values inherited from the elders
- Tamasika – Person indulged in Error, Sleep, Sloth. Mode of Ignorance
- Tulsi – Holy basil plant. In her human form, she was Vrinda

- Upanishads – Hindu scriptures that impart religious knowledge
- Vaishno Devi – Goddess Durga
- Vishnu – Lord Vishnu (Krishna , Rama are incarnations of Lord Vishnu)
- Vedas – Oldest religious scriptures of Hindus
- Vrindavan – A place in north India where Lord spent all His childhood in his last incarnation as Krishna
- Yagyas – Acts performed for sacrifice
- Yogi – Person leading a life full of sacrifice
- Yashoda – Mother of Lord Krishna

THE STERLING BOOK OF

Unity in Diversity
O.P. Ghai
ISBN 978 81 207 3739 6

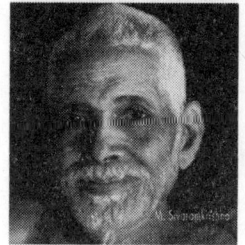

Ramana Maharishi
M. Sivaramkrishna
ISBN 978 81 207 3788 4

Buddha and His Teachings
Kingsley Heendeniya
ISBN 1 8455 7 168 1

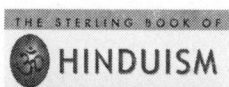

Hinduism
Dr Karan Singh
ISBN 1 84557 425 7

Bhagavad Gita
O P Ghai
ISBN 1 84557 426 5

Indian Classical Dance
Shovana Narayan
ISBN 1 84557 169 X

Ma Sarada
Prof M Sivaramkrishna
ISBN 1 84557 203 3

Selections from the Qur'an
O.P. Ghai
ISBN 978 81 207 6154 4

Essence of Indian Thought
Baldeo Sahai
ISBN 81 207 5348 8

Essence of Sufism
Sheikh Taoshobuddha
ISBN 978 81 207 5694 6